Praise for *Virtual*

"Think about the most useful book you've ever read. It will now become the second most useful. Ducker says work and success only breed more work and success, and he couldn't be more right. This is the field guide for building a team, out-sourcing, and taking back control of your life."

—JAY BAER, *New York Times* bestselling author of *Youtility*

"If you could buy a turnkey solution to your most vexing busi-ness problem, this is it. Chris Ducker explains exactly how to get more done in less time—and, as a bonus, get back the life you gave up when you decided to go into business for yourself. Virtual assistants are the key, and *Virtual Freedom* gives you everything you need to know."

—MICHAEL HYATT, *New York Times* bestselling author of *Platform*

"Chris Ducker passionately teaches freedom. His manifesto is a wake-up call for all entrepreneurs seeking to take back more of their time—in business and life. Cheers to your inspiration!"

—MICHAEL COVEL, bestselling author of *Trend Following*

"Set your ideas free, and you'll think bigger. Set your entire work system free, and you'll grow bigger. Chris Ducker is on to something here. Get in fast!"

—CHRIS BROGAN, *New York Times* bestselling author of *Trust Agents*

"Who would you rather trust to learn about building a virtual team, to help grow your business? Someone who 'talks' about outsourcing or someone who LIVES it? Chris Ducker lives it—every day—and this book proves it!"

—DEREK HALPERN, founder of SocialTriggers.com

"Countless business owners are getting bogged down dealing with mundane tasks. As a result, they sacrifice their freedom and even their happiness dealing with stuff they shouldn't be. The master of how to break free from this, Chris Ducker, has the book you NEED to read. He takes the fear out of virtualizing your business and shows you how to live your life while your business works for YOU!"

—PETER SHANKMAN, bestselling author of *Nice Companies Finish First*

"Chris, thank you for the inspiration and direction you provide on a daily basis; this book shall become the bible on how to build your dream business without working yourself into an early grave!"

—JOHN LEE DUMAS, host and founder of Entrepreneur on Fire

"Time, not money, is our most precious asset. In *Virtual Freedom*, Ducker gives incredibly practical, proven advice for getting our time back so we can live a life of true freedom with the most luxurious of luxuries: choice over what we do with our time. Read it and prepare to be free."

—KATE NORTHRUP, bestselling author of *Money: A Love Story*

"When it comes to the world of virtual staffing, Chris Ducker is the real deal. His framework for outsourcing elements of your daily life will help your business thrive. The world needs this book, and I'm glad it's finally been written!"

—SRINIVAS RAO, host and founder of BlogCastFM

"Your small business won't grow without a team behind you. Chris Ducker has written a step-by-step guide to building and managing a virtual team machine. Follow his framework and watch your enterprise grow into your dream business."

—MELINDA EMERSON, bestselling author of *Become Your Own Boss in 12 Months*

"The world of business no longer has borders or cubicle walls to get in the way of anyone, anywhere in the world from building the successful business they've always dreamed of. Chris Ducker lives what is between these pages and you'd be hard pressed to find a happier and successful entrepreneur out there! Stop giving up on your dreams and begin living them!"

—C.C. CHAPMAN, CMO, YSN

"Have you ever read a book that you just couldn't put down because you simply need to know what's on the next page? *Virtual Freedom* did that for me, because what Chris has produced in this book will literally change your business, and your life!"

—PAT FLYNN, bestselling author of *Let Go*

"The biggest challenge entrepreneurs face when building their business is acknowledging they can't do everything themselves. The second biggest challenge is understanding what to hand over, who to hire, and how to handle that transition. Thankfully this has all been distilled into this amazing book—one that I wish had been available when I was starting out!"

—NATALIE SISSON, bestselling author of *Suitcase Entrepreneur*

"In a world where TIME is becoming more and more precious, it's refreshing to see a book that helps us get back what so many of us have lost in the day to day rigors of the demanding business world we're all now a part of. Chris Ducker is a true pioneer in this exploding field, and *Virtual Freedom* is a must read for anyone that is looking for a clear plan and strategy to get back more time so they can enjoy doing the things that bring them the greatest joy."

—MARCUS SHERIDAN, author, speaker, and "sales lion"

"If you're trying to build a more focused business and want to free up massive amounts of time, get this book!"

—DAVE CRENSHAW, author of *The Focused Business*

"After spending the first year of my business working fourteen to eighteen hours a day, seven days a week, it became clear that I could no longer attempt to do everything on my own. Perhaps it was the week in the hospital following that year that gave me the wake-up call that I needed. My life changed within months of hiring my first virtual assistant. Chris Ducker has written the book that I wish had existed when I first got involved with virtual assistants—it would have made my life so much easier. If you are considering hiring a virtual assistant, this book is a must read!"

—CLIFF RAVENSCRAFT, broadcaster, PodcastAnswerman.com

"I'm not going to lie; my business used to be a stress-fest until I unleashed the power of outsourcing on it. It literally changed my entire business world and now I can work when, where, and how I want. When it comes to learning how to do this, there's no better expert than Chris Ducker, and no better bible than *Virtual Freedom*."

—DAVID SITEMAN GARLAND, mediapreneur and host of
The Rise to the Top

"I wish I had this book when I was struggling to be a superhero in my own business. Chris completely gets where I was at back then, and it wasn't pretty. Please read this book. Twice. This is a must read for any overloaded entrepreneur."

—CHRIS GARRETT, bestselling co-author of *ProBlogger*

"Every entrepreneur needs to understand the importance of utilizing and leveraging great talent—no matter where it is in the world. Chris Ducker has written a book that is going to change the mindset of an entire generation of entrepreneurs. It's a total game changer!"

—LEWIS HOWES, World Record Holder and Instigator of Greatness

"I have referred a number of people over to Chris for information on how to find and get started with a virtual assistant. For me, he is the "go to" expert. I tell them he pretty much wrote the book on the topic. And now ... he quite literally has.

I suggest you read it and apply every word. One thing I know from experience is that outsourcing IS the path to freedom as an entrepreneur, regardless of what level you're at."

—DAVID RISLEY, founder of Blog Marketing Academy

"Why get bogged down in administration when you can focus on building your business? Chris Ducker provides a book that's essential for every entrepreneur out there. If you want to free up your valuable time and increase profits in your business, buy this book!"

—IAN CLEARY, publisher, RazorSocial.com

"This is a book for a new world of business, where technology—not subways or planes or cars—connects people to their offices and team members to each other. It offers you a prescription that'll lead you to a more flexible, efficient, and (ultimately) more productive business. As well as a happier life! Which is no small thing at all!"

—ANN HANDLEY, bestselling co-author of *Content Rules*

"The best question to ask yourself when determining a book's worth is 'Has the author earned the right?' Chris has owned and operated a virtual staffing company for every second of the ten years I've known him. For me, he's not just an expert in the space—he helped create the space!"

—COREY PERLMAN, author of *eBoot Camp* and
Social Media Overload

"*Virtual Freedom* is the answer to 'now what?' *The E-Myth* and *The 4-Hour Workweek* told us that we need to work on our businesses, not in them. In many ways, we were left to figure out what was next. In this book, Chris Ducker holds your hand and gives you the steps and confidence to follow the path he's taken and others like him, as you make the transition from wannapreneur to a successful business owner with true freedom!"

—PHIL TAYLOR, director, Financial Bloggers Conference

"As an entrepreneur, I look for leverage points. The bigger the lever, the less work I have to do and the faster and easier success becomes. Outsourcing is one of those massive levers I've been using—in great part, thanks to Chris Ducker. If you're interested in gaining the ultimate leverage for your business, *Virtual Freedom* is simply a MUST read!"

—GIDEON SHALWICK, founder, Splasheo.com

"Chris Ducker passionately teaches freedom. His manifesto is a wake-up call for all entrepreneurs seeking to take back more of their time—in business and life. Cheers to your inspiration!"

—MICHAEL COVEL, bestselling author of *Trend Following*

"*Virtual Freedom* offers THE solution for entrepreneurs who are trying to build a serious business that isn't fully dependent on them. It's as if the book holds you by the hand and guides you through building an empire of greatness. I wish someone knocked me over the head with this book in 2008! Reading it will change many lives for the better."

—LESLIE SAMUEL, owner, BecomeABlogger.com

"Chris clearly knows from experience how overwhelming it can be to run a small business, but he now knows something most of us don't: how to master the art of outsourcing. Thankfully, he tells all in his new book *Virtual Freedom*. If you have a small business, you are losing time and money if you don't read this book."

—JAIME TARDY, author of *The Eventual Millionaire*

"People have been talking about virtual teammates for years, but with Chris's *Virtual Freedom*, we finally have a guide to the hiring, training, and managing them. Chris is one of the preeminent thought leaders on virtual staffing and provides an excellent resource for people wanting to build a scalable, profitable, and effective business that blends virtual and local staff."

—CHARLIE GILKEY, bestselling author of *The Small Business Lifecycle*

"Chris is endlessly impressive with how many things he gets done; running a blog/podcast and other social media channels as well as an incredibly successful business, visiting and talking at and even organizing conferences, and passionately helping others achieve something similar—all while having three children! This book explains how he can outsource tasks he doesn't enjoy as much or that others would do better, so that he can be the best CEO, and dad, he could possibly be. A must on every businessperson's reading list!"

—BENNY LEWIS, author of *Fluent in 3 Months*

"There are probably things you're doing every day that are limiting your impact and fracturing your focus. In *Virtual Freedom*, Chris offers a more effective, sane way to operate your business and your life."

—TODD HENRY, author of *Die Empty*

"At first, the amount of impressive work Chris Ducker is able to accomplish seems superhuman. Blogging, podcasting, writing books, managing a 200+ person company, running a co-working space—he does it all. But then you realize he has a secret … Chris uses a small army of virtual staff to make these superhuman feats possible. Luckily, through the pages of *Virtual Freedom*, Chris is sharing his secrets with the rest of us! Read this book to get your own superhuman powers!"

—CORBETT BARR, co-founder, Fizzle.co

"My first digital product took six months to create because I thought I had to do it all. Today, I produce products in a fraction of the time—thanks to my virtual staff! What Chris Ducker preaches in *Virtual Freedom* is true—success isn't about longer hours, it's about leverage—and his book gives you the tools you need to leverage worldwide talent to build your business!"

—JAMES WEDMORE, online publisher digital entrepreneur at JamesWedmore.com

"Being your own boss can be a blessing and a curse. On good days you feel like you can conquer the world, but on bad days you're exhausted by the never-ending list of tasks that have bottlenecked on your to-do list. In *Virtual Freedom*, Chris Ducker saves the day with practical, actionable tips for business owners everywhere on how to best leverage the rapidly expanding global workforce. You don't have to go it alone. This book is the blueprint you need to go from a stressed-out, overworked entrepreneur to radically transforming your business and life."

—JENNY BLAKE, international speaker and author of *Life After College*

"Long hours, time away from the family, and very few vacation days are often 'the norm' when you're running your own business. However, it doesn't need to be that way. *Virtual Freedom* is the first book of its kind, showing you exactly how to free yourself from doing everything, instead giving you the step-by-step roadmap to build a virtual team that can literally explode your success and give you back your freedom. Chris himself experienced the burnout that you might be feeling at this very moment, and therefore each page of this book is rooted in personal experience and life lessons. If you want more freedom in your life to do what you love the most, you must read this book."

—AMY PORTERFIELD, co-author of *Facebook Marketing All-in-One for Dummies*

"When it comes to outsourcing and business freedom, there is no comparison to Chris Ducker. If you desire a lifestyle business, read this book TODAY!"

—RYAN LEE, author of *The Millionaire Workout*

VIRTUAL FREEDOM

HOW TO WORK WITH VIRTUAL STAFF TO BUY MORE TIME, BECOME MORE PRODUCTIVE, AND BUILD YOUR DREAM BUSINESS

Chris Ducker

BenBella Books
Dallas, TX

BenBella

BenBella Books, Inc.
10300 N. Central Expressway, Suite #530 | Dallas, TX 75231
www.benbellabooks.com | Send feedback to feedback@benbellabooks.com

Printed in the United States of America
10 9 8 7 6 5 4 3 2 1

Library of Congress Cataloging-in-Publication Data
Ducker, Chris.
  Virtual freedom : how to work with virtual staff to buy more time,
become more productive, and build your dream business / by Chris
Ducker.
      pages cm
  Includes bibliographical references and index.
  ISBN 978-1-939529-74-9 (trade paper : alk. paper) — ISBN 978-1-
939529-75-6 (electronic) 1. Virtual reality in management. 2. Virtual
work teams—Management. I. Title.
  HD30.2122.D83 2014
  658.4'022—dc23

                                                              2013039792

Editing by Amy Hochstein | Copyediting by Shannon Kelly
Proofreading by Amy Zarkos and James Fraleigh
Indexing by Jigsaw Indexing
Cover design by Bradford Foltz | Jacket design by Sarah Dombrowsky
Text design and composition by Silver Feather Design
Printed by Bang Printing

Distributed by Perseus Distribution | www.perseusdistribution.com
To place orders through Perseus Distribution:
Tel: 800-343-4499 | Fax: 800-351-5073
E-mail: orderentry@perseusbooks.com

Significant discounts for bulk sales are available. Please contact Glenn
Yeffeth at glenn@benbellabooks.com or 214-750-3628.

SEP 1 6 2014

To my children, CJ, Chloe, and Charles, I love you more than anything else in this world. You are all the inspiration I need to get up early every day and continue to work hard on my own entrepreneurial freedom.

To my wife, Ercille. Thank you for supporting me, motivating me, and encouraging me in everything I do. Most importantly, thank you for being my best friend.
I love you.

Contents

Introduction 1

    Superhero Syndrome 1
    Becoming a Virtual CEO 3
    It's Time to Make a Choice 7
    Why Build a Virtual Team in the First Place? 8
    Getting Started with This Book 9

SECTION ONE: Finding and Hiring Your Virtual Staff 13

    The Fundamentals 14
    Reality Check: The Myth of the Super-VA 15
    Introducing the General Virtual Assistant (GVA) 16
    Creating Your 3 Lists to Freedom 20
    Getting Ready to Start 24
    Understanding the 2 Different Types
        of Outsourcing 25
    Freedom Spotlight: Jared Croslow,
        Cliconomics.com 27
    Defining the Different Types of Virtual Workers 28
    Case Study #1: Todd Beuckens, Elllo 38
    Finding the Right Virtual Staff 42

The 10 Elements of a Good Job Description   47

Case Study #2: Tom Libelt, Libelty SEO   52

The Interview Process
    (and the 10 Questions You Should Ask)   55

Confidentiality and Contracts   60

NDAs (Nondisclosure Agreements)   62

SECTION TWO: Training Your Virtual Staff   63

The Biggest Problem with Training
    Virtual Workers: You!   64

Case Study #3: Tristan King, Shopify Ninjas   70

Get to Know Your VAs   73

Develop Your Training Tools:
    The VA Training Trifecta   74

Case Study #4: Kyle Zimmerman,
    Kyle Zimmerman Photography   80

Best Practices When Training
    Your Virtual Staff   84

Throw Your VA a Curveball   86

Your VA Success Equation   88

Freedom Spotlight: Pat Flynn,
    SmartPassiveIncome.com   91

SECTION THREE: Managing Your Virtual Staff   93

Don't Be a Virtual Vulture   94

Case Study #5: Steve Dixon, Dixon Clothing Group
    and Breakthrough4Business   101

How to Manage Different VA Roles   103

CONTENTS

The Difference Between Revolving
    Tasks and Projects 114
Using Project-Management Software 118
Reports from Your Virtual Staff 121
Freedom Spotlight: Justin Fulcher, Kinda IT 125
Paying and Motivating Your Virtual Staff 126

SECTION FOUR: The Big Question: Stay Local or Go Overseas? 133

The Advantages of Staying Closer to Home 134
Why Outsourcing Overseas Is Not for Everyone—
    or Every Business 138
What About Customer Support? 140
The Outsourcing Destination of Choice:
    The Philippines 141
Case Study #6: Fiona Lewis, Super Savvy Business ... 144
5 Things to Remember When Working
    with Filipino VAs 148
Case Study #7: Paul Holland, VideoTise 153

SECTION FIVE: The Next Level: Building Your Virtual Team 159

How Different Types of Virtual Employees
    Will Work Together 160
Case Study #8: Nate Ginsburg, Onset LLC 178
Setting Company Goals and Rewards 181
Meeting Everyone in Person 183
Setting Up a Social Network for Your Virtual Team ... 186

Freedom Spotlight: Joe Daniel,
The Football-Defense Report 188
When to Create the Virtual Project Manager Role 189

SECTION SIX: The Case for Content 199

Why Your Business Needs to Produce
Online Content Consistently 203
What Is "Good" Content? 209
The P2P (People-to-People) Philosophy 212
Case Study #9: Joshua Van Den Broek,
Fitco Health Technologies 214
The Importance of Being Remembered 218
Getting Your Virtual Team to Do
(Almost) All the Work for You 218
Freedom Spotlight: Natalie Sisson,
The Suitcase Entrepreneur 229

SECTION SEVEN: Time to Get Started 233

Your First Six Months 234

Conclusion 237

BONUS SECTION: Top 10 Virtual Team-Building
Mistakes (and How to Avoid Them!) 239

Resources 255
Gratitude 265
About the Author 267
Index 269

Introduction

Superhero Syndrome

A radioactive spider accidentally slipped into the backpack of high school student Peter Parker and delivered a life-changing bite. Peter didn't know it at the time, but this moment was the birth of the Amazing Spider-Man.

At first, Peter's gifts were nothing more than a novelty, allowing him to become a quasi-television star and make some easy cash. But as he soon discovered, *with great power comes great responsibility*. As an entrepreneur, the same is true of you.

You and I may not know exactly when it happened, but you, too, were bitten. Chances are the bite wasn't from a radioactive spider, but it was just as potent—and just as transformative. It was the bite of the entrepreneurial bug.

For some of you, this bite came in the form of a life-altering event, such as accidentally creating a new product or service, inheriting a family business, or getting laid off. Whatever happened, you developed powerful skills and abilities as a consequence.

Your superhero powers probably consist of

- the ability to see opportunities that others don't

- the drive and energy to work fourteen-hour days
- the courage to approach strangers and share your ideas
- the dexterity to morph into the different roles your business needs

These powers are a blessing because you have the potential to impact countless lives with your vision and innovation. At the same time, your powers are a curse because you can easily be deceived into thinking you can travel down the entrepreneurial road alone.

Welcome, my friend, to superhero syndrome. Your symptoms will no doubt include the following:

- If there's any money to be saved in doing something yourself, you'll do it.
- If you don't know how to do something, you'll teach yourself.
- You may have the inability to take criticism of any kind.
- You'll believe that your ideas and concepts are far greater than anyone else's.
- The word "recharge" will only apply to your cell phone.

After all, your business is your baby, and who better to take care of that baby than the person who gave birth to it—you! However, this will all eventually catch up with you, and the strength that you possess as an entrepreneur will start to backfire. Your superpowers will ultimately begin to control you, eating away at your energy levels and stumping any potential for freedom in your life. They will leave you stressed and overworked, and ultimately you will be no good to anyone or anything—including your business.

Becoming a Virtual CEO

You might assume that as an ambassador of virtual staffing, my professional journey has always been lined with an army of virtual assistants (VAs) doing the work while I strategize and delegate from a remote location wearing flip-flops and a Tommy Bahama shirt. As sexy as that may sound, it is not my story.

Reaching Burnout

In 2008, I started an outsourcing call center in the Philippines. Live2Sell, Inc. focused on outbound lead generation and inbound customer support for small- to medium-size businesses. By the end of that year, we had grown from a small provider with just seven staff members to a full-fledged call center of seventy-five full-time employees.

My workdays had progressively risen from eleven hours to sometimes sixteen hours a day. Even that amount of work and energy dedicated to the business wasn't enough to keep up with the workflow demands—and that's when my own superhero syndrome began to kick in. I believed I could fill every role in my growing business. No matter how much time, energy, or talent something required, I was up for the challenge. I thought there was an unlimited supply of time and energy within me.

At this point in the story, my wife gave birth to our son,

Charlie—making us a family of five. I did what I could to help out with the daily responsibilities at home while carrying on working long, crazy hours. In late 2009, I found myself burnt out and stressed like never before. I woke up one day and realized something startling: I really didn't *have* a company. I *was* the company!

Something needed to change.

Firing Myself

The Greek philosopher Plato said, "Necessity is the mother of invention." If you think about it for a moment, that statement can clarify a lot:

- It's the reason that people miraculously get work done at the last minute—because they need to.
- It's the reason that some of your best ideas surface when you're faced with a do-or-die situation—because you must come up with something or face terrible consequences.
- It's the reason that my good friend Pat Flynn, creator of the online brand Smart Passive Income, found success as a digital entrepreneur after being laid off from his job as an architect—because he had to.

And it's the reason that yours truly, Chris Ducker, chose to fire himself from the role of burnt-out micromanaging CEO—because I needed to. It was the best thing for me and the best thing for the business. The simple fact was that I could no longer work such crazy hours while also maintaining a healthy role as a husband and father of three. So I fired myself.

I fired myself from thinking that more of my time and energy was the solution to every problem. I fired myself from being a micromanager, which was causing a bottleneck in a lot of our day-to-day operations. I fired myself from building the business on my shoulders and instead chose to build it around a system of highly skilled local and virtual employees.

I'm not saying I fired myself from working, nor am I saying there's anything wrong with work. What I am saying is that I fired myself from specific roles within my organization—roles that were better suited for someone else. This also meant I had to resign certain ways of thinking.

I had to stop believing I would somehow work my way to freedom or that I was only being productive if I was busy doing something. My own superhero syndrome had gotten to the point where I realized that I had to start believing in my staff more in order to allow them to do their jobs without my micromanaging getting in the way of their personal development.

The reality is that work and success only create more work and success, so I devised a plan to become a virtual CEO by the end of 2010 and decided to blog about my journey on a regular basis under the banner of Virtual Business Lifestyle, which is now ChrisDucker.com.

I began with small steps, such as

- taking myself out of the massive amount of e-mail threads I was copied into
- hiring additional virtual assistants to manage day-to-day administrative jobs, such as replying to inquiries

- hiring a full-time trainer for new recruits instead of handling the training myself
- developing an internal management team
- setting benchmarks and clearly defined tasks instead of micromanaging
- hiring experienced online marketers and other virtual staff to help me with business development and lead generation

Turning these smaller steps into monthly goals made them much easier to attain.

While some goals were easy to hit, others had to be shifted around. For example, when I hired an operations manager, I had to delve back into the training department because my trainer needed additional training herself!

So, what happened?

The Outcome

By the end of 2010, my management team and I had completely systematized the business. I went from working six days a week for twelve to sixteen hours each day to instead putting in the equivalent of just one or two full working days spread out over the entire week.

I had completely flipped the script in my business and could now say I was a business owner instead of saying I was owned by a business. It was, and continues to be, a great feeling.

With the extra time and more efficient systems I had created, I was able to launch another endeavor—Virtual Staff Finder, a professional VA matchmaking service. I also

began consistently producing online content at a completely new level. This content is now syndicated on multiple
media platforms:

- **my blog**: ChrisDucker.com
- **my podcast**: NewBusinessPodcast.com
- **my YouTube channel**: YouTube.com/ChrisDucker
- **social media channels**: Twitter.com/ChrisDucker
  and Facebook.com/ChrisDuckerDotCom

Every one of these activities and the additional opportunities that come my way, such as coaching, advising, in-
vesting, and speaking engagements, would not be possible
without the involvement of someone from my team.

It's Time to Make a Choice

So what about you? Did anything about my story sound
familiar? Are you working yourself ragged with no end in
sight? Has your own superhero syndrome reared its ugly
little head yet?

The way I see it, you have a choice to make: break down
or build your team.

I'm not saying you'll break down immediately or that
you can't work seven days a week for fourteen hours each
day. However, a time will come when something has to give.
Working such long hours could affect a personal relationship, force you to lose an important client, or even cause
serious health issues.

The choice is yours. For now, I just want you to keep
reading.

Why Build a Virtual Team in the First Place?

To some, the concept of hiring and working with people that they will likely never meet in person is as foreign as it comes. However, the fact is that the world—particularly the business world—has changed drastically in the last ten to fifteen years.

The Internet has enabled us not only to do business from a distance, but also to capitalize on an avalanche of global talent that was previously inaccessible.

Sure, there are some downfalls to working with virtual staff, such as different time zones, the inability to meet in person regularly, and the potential of cultural differences, but when handled correctly, the pros far outweigh the cons. These pros include

- cost-saving benefits, especially if working with overseas staff
- hiring without geographical constraints
- quick and easy hiring for one-time jobs
- minimal physical office requirements

All this being said, many first-time outsourcers fear that because they are at a distance from their virtual employees they're going to be taken advantage of in some way. It's a fair assumption, and one that does come true for some. However, it's my job as the author of this book to show you how to do this thing right from the outset: to limit the obvious trial and error that comes with any hiring situation, whether physical or virtual, and to ultimately help you fall in love with your virtual staff, the way that I have and the way that others have, too.

Those others include Leslie Samuel, a full-time university professor who moonlights as an equally full-time online entrepreneur. When Leslie first started his business, he was teaching during the day and a slave to his new business in the evening. His marriage suffered. His health suffered. In fact, almost every aspect of his life suffered. After putting in place several systems and ultimately hiring a VA to run his small online business for him, things got easier. Leslie now says that hiring a VA saved not only his business but also his life. Pretty strong stuff.

Another entrepreneur that has injected virtual staff into his business is thought leader Michael Hyatt. He started hiring virtual assistants when he became overwhelmed by his blog's incredible popularity, which freed up time for him to focus on what he really enjoyed—writing.

You'll discover plenty more stories like Leslie's and Michael's throughout this book—stories of business owners who work with the help of virtual assistants all over the world. You'll meet, for example, Kyle Zimmerman, who owns and operates a retail photography studio in New Mexico, and Natalie Sisson, who has literally lived out of her suitcase for years as she builds an online business. Through the case studies and spotlights in this book, entrepreneurs just like you share their struggles of working with virtual staff and how they overcame those struggles.

Getting Started with This Book

Before we dive into the world of virtual assistants—which I'll also refer to as VAs, virtual workers, freelancers, virtual staff, outsourcers, and virtual employees (plus a few other terms) throughout this book—let's clarify exactly whom this book is for and what you can expect to learn.

The last thing I want to imply is that virtual employees are only for a certain type of person or business: far from it. This book is for solopreneurs with a bootstrap budget, it's for bloggers and other types of digital entrepreneurs, and it's for freelancers who wear all the hats in their businesses and want to stop driving themselves mad. It's written with both brick-and-mortar businesses and e-commerce businesses in mind: for example, the small-town store owner who would like to use the power of the Internet to market his or her business and bring new clients on board, and the online business owner looking to expand market reach. Every entrepreneur who wants to free up more time, become more productive, and drastically increase his or her business growth and profits will benefit from this book.

Instead of me telling you to sit back and relax while I teach you something, I need you to get ready to work. Some of what we'll discuss will sound completely logical, and you'll be nodding your head in agreement. Other points will sound entirely unattractive and unnecessary, and you may think, "It won't be that big a deal if I skip this part. Chris won't mind."

Stop! Don't think that for even one moment—because Chris *will* mind.

Every activity and concept in this book has been tried, tested, and experienced by myself and many other real entrepreneurs—people working on real projects and building real businesses with real virtual staff and real money.

This book is not about simple tactics that allow you to outsource a few tasks here and there. It's about building an engine, my friend. An engine that will turn your four-cylinder business into a twin-turbo race car.

Does that mean my methods can't be tailored to better fit your specific needs? Of course not. But in order to customize my strategies, you first have to learn and use the strategies. For now, it's important that you follow through on every activity. You'll be 100 percent student, and I'll be 100 percent virtual teacher. That's something I don't take lightly. I promise not to waste your time with useless information, unnecessary repetition, or cheap anecdotes; there's nothing I hate more than a fluffy book with little meat.

Things to Keep in Mind

Here's a simple concept I'd like you to keep in mind as you begin or continue your journey towards virtual freedom:

Rome wasn't built in a day—it also took more than one person to build it!

It's a learning process and a building process to stop struggling to do it all on your own. As you become more fluent in the virtual business lifestyle, some concepts and ideas will fall easily into place. Others will need to be customized to your needs.

When you're done reading this book, you'll have the blueprint you need to go from a stressed-out, overworked business owner to someone who is refocused and highly energized about all the new freedom you've amassed. You'll enjoy the prospect of building your business again instead of just running it.

Remember when you first opened your doors to customers? The energy you felt getting to work every day? The buzz you got from talking about your business to everyone and anyone you met?

I'm going to restore all of that original enthusiasm and help you prepare for the next ten years of blossoming into the most successful entrepreneur you can be. And it will all result from the strategy of building and utilizing a virtual team to help you run, support, and grow your business.

Shall we begin?

SECTION ONE

Finding and Hiring Your Virtual Staff

There aren't too many differences between finding and hiring virtual workers and doing the same with employees that will be based in your office. However, the differences that do exist are important to understand.

There's a lot to cover in this section, and we'll focus particularly on the following topics:

- understanding the myth of the super-VA (and busting it!)
- how creating your "3 Lists to Freedom" will change everything
- the different types of virtual workers and how they can help you
- how and where to find the right virtual staff
- ten interview questions you need to ask when hiring

Before you dive in, let's get a general overview of the game and learn about the ins and outs of the playing field.

The Fundamentals

Just like in sports, we need to begin with the fundamentals. Once you understand these principles, you can tailor your approach to streamline the process. And this is a process—one that should be followed step by step.

Here are the basic rules of the game:

1. **Your virtual workers are people, not a program.** Though communication with your virtual staff takes place via e-mail and web-based audio and/or video chat services like Skype, VAs still deserve the same respect you would give any human being. It's in your best interest to understand each worker's communication customs and to be aware of his or her cultural holidays and traditions.

2. **Put quality in, get quality out.** The quality of work you receive from virtual employees is proportional to the quality of the instructions they receive. Are your instructions clear and concise? Or are you giving them a jumbled mess of instructions and hoping they can connect the dots?

3. **One size does not fit all.** All VAs have strengths and weaknesses, but they may not want to tell you that. They want to please you and will try to figure out ways to do whatever you want. This is a double-edged sword. Take care to match the right VA to each of your needs. We'll go into this in a lot more detail.

4. **Super-VAs don't exist.** There is no one virtual assistant anywhere on the planet who can handle everything you need help with in your business. Think about it: When your roof is leaking, you don't ask your electrician to pop around and fix it. You call a roofing expert to come over and do the necessary repairs. This is one of the biggest myths in virtual staffing so I will discuss this in more detail below, but bottom line: hire for the role, not for the task.

Now that you know the rules of the game, we can get to work!

Reality Check: The Myth of the Super-VA

The idea of a super-VA is the big kahuna—the one mistake that I see entrepreneurs who are getting started with outsourcing make over and over again. Read these words carefully: there's no such thing as a super-VA. It drives me crazy when an entrepreneur sets out to find that one special VA who can do all of the work in his or her business. I can't tell you how many requests we receive at Virtual Staff Finder from entrepreneurs who are looking for VAs who can handle all of the following tasks and more:

- update blog posts
- manage social media
- edit video
- transcribe audio

- create custom images and icons
- design and develop websites
- respond to customer support tickets
- research and recruit affiliates
- do Amazon shopping for birthday gifts for loved ones

There's nothing wrong with trying to outsource a scattered group of tasks and projects, but a single VA is not your answer. As a business owner, I can relate to the multiple hats entrepreneurs need to wear in order to get things done. However, filling your business with more entrepreneurial types who also think that they can do it all is the last thing you should do. Your focus needs to shift from finding a super-VA to identifying the specific roles your business needs to fill.

Remember, empire-building equals team-building—and you have to identify the positions your team needs before you begin recruiting the players.

Introducing the
General Virtual Assistant (GVA)

I've had the pleasure of speaking on stage and working with business owners from all around the world on the subject of virtual staffing and outsourcing. No matter where I am or who I'm working with, my basic message remains the same: Every entrepreneur needs a GVA!

Even though the super-VA doesn't exist, the general virtual assistant is about as close to one as you can get. They can't wear all of the different VA hats out there, but GVAs will help you run your life and maximize your productivity by freeing you of time-draining, repetitive tasks that no business owner should be handling. Your GVA is your sidekick. Batman had Robin. Sherlock Holmes had Watson. Hardy had Laurel. Michael Jordan had Scottie Pippen.

Working with a GVA is the first step to realizing the power of virtual staffing. Your GVA will immediately begin saving you time and allowing you to work *on* your business instead of being trapped working *in* it.

Are you struggling to stay up to date with or roll out the following types of tasks on a regular basis?

- researching competitors' websites for lists of products and prices
- compiling a list of local events that you could sponsor or where you could exhibit
- combing your blog's analytics to find out which pages or blog posts are receiving the most traffic
- keeping your social media channels updated and interesting for followers
- getting featured in local, national, and industry-related press
- transcribing your online videos and podcast episodes to use as future e-books and in infographics to promote your products and services
- keeping your calendar updated so you don't miss an important golf date with your top client

Delegating these small tasks begins freeing up extra time for you each day. Ten minutes here and thirty minutes there can add up quickly. Delegating also gets rid of all those unresolved items you're carrying around in your head. As David

Allen points out in his book *Getting Things Done: The Art of Stress-Free Productivity*, this is one of the critical factors that will allow you to focus.

"Your conscious mind, like a computer screen, is a focusing tool, not a storage place," he writes. "You can think about only two or three things at once. But the incomplete items are being stored in the short-term memory space. And as with RAM (random access memory), there's limited capacity; there's only so much 'stuff' you can store in there and still have that part of your brain functioning at a high level. Most people walk around with their RAM bursting at the seams."

It's crazy how many things you're probably juggling in your head right now. But it's stuff that needs to get done, right? So it has to go somewhere. This is where your superhero syndrome begins to kick in, leading you into thinking that working harder is the solution. But again, the real solution is not longer hours—it's leverage.

As entrepreneurs, time is our most valuable commodity (MVC). Money will come and go, but once you've invested your time into something, that time is gone forever. It stands to reason that if there are any actions we can take as business owners to free up more time in our daily routines, we should take them.

Hiring and working with a GVA will help you do just that. Think of your GVA as a personal assistant (PA). Aside from bringing you a cup of coffee or picking up your dry cleaning, GVAs can do all the same tasks that an old-fashioned, in-office PA could handle.

Here are just a few of the tasks a GVA can take off your

plate so you have more space in your mind and in your workday:

- perform online research
- make online purchases (have the GVA use a prepaid credit card with a small amount you can fund and monitor each month)
- update your calendar
- make a dinner reservation
- draft your latest blog post or upload your You-Tube videos
- send your spouse a gift
- or, if you're single, send e-mails to potential dates on Match.com or eHarmony—yes, really!
- update your Facebook status with prewritten posts
- order more business cards
- collate a list of articles from online news sources and e-mail you with a weekly update
- send a follow-up e-mail or letter to new contacts you just met at that conference you attended
- book your biannual dental cleanings and then update them on your calendar

You'll see that this list is just the beginning of how a GVA can help you achieve freedom on a day-to-day basis. Furthermore, the GVA role is just one of many different types of virtual workers that are out there and ready to be put on your team. The question is, what else can you get virtual assistants to do for you?

You're about to find out, thanks to a very simple, quick, and effective exercise.

Creating Your 3 Lists to Freedom

Your first step toward freedom in any situation is to begin identifying exactly which tasks you want freedom from—and the types of workers you'll need to handle those tasks. This is why at my speaking engagements, in podcast interviews, and even in traditional press appearances on the subject of virtual staffing, I always include my 3 Lists to Freedom exercise. It's incredibly eye-opening, and it gives everyone a customized list of activities to work from as we move along.

Before you start putting together your three lists, let's consider all of the activities you'll need to incorporate. First, take a moment to think about all of the activities your business needs just to maintain itself—these are the day-to-day tasks such as customer service. Next, consider all of the activities needed to grow your business; this might include content creation, for example. Then, go through and highlight the items that you enjoy doing personally. Now you're ready to create your 3 Lists to Freedom.

1. Tasks You Don't Like Doing

This is any task that makes you cringe or procrastinate. Anything can be on this list—except for selling. Selling needs to be one of your top priorities because it's the lifeblood of any business, and no one should know your product or service better than you.

Do you routinely reply to customer service e-mails, perhaps answering the most basic of inquiries? Are you still laying out and formatting your own blog posts? Does this stuff drive you nuts? Put those types of things on this list.

Australian-based James Schramko is one of the most popular Internet marketers operating online today. He is incredibly successful. James started working with virtual assistants to simply handle work that he didn't want to do himself anymore. The result is SuperfastBusiness.com, an extremely systemized online offering with well over fifty (yes, you read that correctly) VAs running his business for him around the clock.

2. Tasks You Don't Know How to Do

Be honest with yourself. Don't let superhero syndrome kick in here. I remember trying to design and develop my first blog on my own using a premium theme. It took me eight hours of work, and I still wasn't happy with it. Why? Because I'm not a bloody web developer, that's why!

Sit back and genuinely think hard about this one. Ask yourself questions such as

- Are there tasks you're currently doing that could be completed faster by someone else?
- Are there projects you're handling that could be wrapped up in a better, more professional way?
- Are you trying to cut costs by dabbling far outside your areas of expertise?

Business coach and podcaster Jaime Tardy hired VAs to manage the web development and online marketing side of her business, EventualMillionaire.com. Why? Because she simply didn't know how to do it herself and admitted the fact, instead of trying to teach herself.

3. Tasks You Feel You Shouldn't Be Doing

This is the list I want you to give the most thought to. It's usually a huge eye-opener for business owners because it gets their internal wheels turning about how they're currently running their businesses. More importantly, this list helps you see how you *want* to be running your business in the future.

Some questions to ponder:

- Which tasks should you simply never touch— meaning you could eliminate them from your schedule entirely, making way for more important tasks?
- Which low-level tasks could be easily given to a virtual assistant as part-time work?
- Which tasks are you handling that could be taken over by a professional who knows exactly what he or she is doing? These are tasks where the potential harm outweighs the cost savings of doing them yourself.
- Which tasks are stopping you from really focusing on the strategic growth of your business?

Mediapreneur David Siteman Garland was bogged down handling every tiny detail in his online media business, TheRiseToTheTop.com. Realizing that he needed more time to focus on the most important things, such as building relationships and further monetizing his blog and online brand, he turned to virtual help. He gained countless hours back into his schedule and today has one of the most popular online TV shows for entrepreneurs.

Here's an example of how your lists might look, as you start out with the exercise. Note: This is standard stuff and generic to entrepreneurs everywhere in today's business world. Your lists should be focused on you and your specific needs as a business owner.

List #1 Don't Like Doing	List #2 Can't Do	List #3 Shouldn't Do
Checking E-mail	Developing Website	Updating Facebook Page
Managing Social Media	Editing Podcast Episodes	Handling Tier 1 Support
Handling Basic Inquiries	Designing Logos & Graphics	Transcribing Online Video
Researching Travel Options	Bookkeeping & Accounts	Managing Company Blog

Keep your 3 Lists to Freedom handy: We'll be coming back to them quite regularly.

*If you'd like to see a video version of this exercise, head over to **ChrisDucker.com/3Lists***

You now have a foundation of tasks that are easily delegated that will continue to grow over time, as they do for most entrepreneurs today—not only that, but through the 3 Lists to Freedom exercise you've deepened your understanding of yourself and the types of tasks you need to delegate. This is essential to your success. With that in mind, let's discuss how to find and hire the people who are going to help revolutionize the way you run and grow your business going forward.

Getting Ready to Start

This is where I begin leading you down the path to virtual freedom, distilling almost ten years of outsourcing experience into a bite-size training system that will revolutionize your personal and professional life.

But before we dive in, I need you to make me a promise. I want you to promise that before you incorporate a single virtual staff member into your workflow or hire additional staff, you will first commit to reading at least the first and second sections of this book. These sections have been specifically designed to point you in the right direction, and they will give you the solid foundation you'll need to build on.

Sure, you might stumble every now and then, but how quickly you pick yourself up and dust yourself off will depend on you consuming the content in these first couple of sections. In my experience, there are two solid reasons why your virtual staffing empire could crumble:

1. **You build around one strong person instead of building a team with specific roles.** This is an easy trap to fall into when you find a VA who works exceptionally well for you. You may think your VA will always be with you

and start building around his or her strengths instead of focusing on building a team. I truly value the longevity of my staff, but I would never put my company in a position where it would be completely destroyed if I lost someone. Each role within your organization should be clearly defined, and you should know exactly what you would do if someone decided to quit or if you needed to let someone go. Life must carry on.

2. **You fail to properly train your team.** Training is the foundation of your success with virtual assistants. You'll learn how to handle this part of the journey in Section 2 of this book.

I want to ensure that you don't make either of those mistakes.

Understanding the 2 Different Types of Outsourcing

In order to simplify things, think of outsourcing as falling into two different categories: project-based outsourcing and role-based outsourcing.

- **Project-based outsourcing** is used when a business needs just one task or one project completed. This might be a simple task like creating a logo or installing an auto-responder form on a website, or it could be a more detailed project like creating an e-commerce site or a mobile app.
- **Role-based outsourcing** involves finding someone

to fill a particular role within your business on a part-time or full-time basis. In role-based outsourcing, the VA becomes a member of your team. In order for this to make financial sense, you'll need to have enough work to justify paying someone regularly to perform these tasks.

The upside to having a full-time or part-time employee on your team is the speed at which you'll be able to implement everything you want to do. But what if you don't have enough work or revenue to support a full-time or part-time virtual employee?

Great question. For now, you'll need to work with a project-based mindset but keep a long-term perspective. This means each task you outsource is an opportunity to

- **Learn how to properly communicate the work you want to delegate.** Save any correspondence or media that could be used to train future VAs. There's no reason to reinvent the wheel.
- **Find a VA you might want to work with in the future on a part-time or full-time basis.** Some of the best working relationships will arise out of working on smaller tasks together. Keep an eye out for promising talent that you'd like to bring on board in the future.

Whether you start on a smaller scale with freelancers on a task-by-task basis or you get started with a team of part-time or full-time workers, one thing is for sure—you had better understand who should be doing what for you.

Jared Croslow
Long-Time Internet Marketer
Cliconomics.com

Jared Croslow is a brilliant marketer. A true entrepreneur, through and through. His thirst for building businesses, creating great products and services, and generally helping everyone he comes into contact with is second to none.

❯ The Problem

When I first spoke with Jared in 2011, he was working with five full-time VAs on various ventures, including his Internet marketing blog, Cliconomics .com. On more than one occasion, Jared realized that although he was certainly not short on staff, he was short on projects and tasks for them to work on. Even with the support that he had in place, Jared was operating his business on what he now calls the "just in time" model, where he would stress himself out trying to come up with tasks for his staff to do—aptly capturing the anxiety that comes along with trying to manage every aspect of your business by yourself. He now recognizes that this is not a healthy, successful way to go about business; in fact, it's a good way to exhaust yourself and make mistakes due to a lack of expertise.

❯ The Solution

Jared decided to switch up his business plan and hire VAs on a task-by-task basis. He now operates his business using what he calls the "just in case" model. This model entails hiring several part-time VAs to do the necessary work but only when it needs to be done. For example, he has hired VAs to aid in the design and development of a new tactic—hiring simply "just in case" he needs to.

27

> **The Outcome**

Jared's business is far more successful since he has made this shift in the way that he runs his virtual staffing plans—and his VAs are far more satisfied with their productivity.

Defining the Different Types of Virtual Workers

The moment you experience the power of a specialized, well-trained team of VAs, you'll have access to one of the most powerful assets any entrepreneur can wish for—more time.

Just imagine what it would be like to have more time to work *on* your business instead of constantly working *in* the business. In order to get there, you must first begin by defining the roles your business needs to fill.

This is where your answers from the 3 Lists to Freedom exercise will come in handy. See, I told you we'd be seeing that again! My recommendation is to continually refer back to this list and use it as the framework for building your virtual team. When it comes to building a real team of your own, a team that becomes just as important to your business as the very customers that it serves, I consistently use the mantra, "Hire for the role, not for the task."

Let's take a look at the various VA roles, including typical duties within these roles and some rough pay scales. To make things easy to follow, keep in mind that these pay scales reflect a full-time (eight hours a day, Monday through Friday) position for an overseas virtual assistant. I've decided to base the figures on Filipino VAs because that's the demographic I know personally, so please keep this in mind as well.

For part-time roles, simply cut the salary guidelines in half. Please note, however, that almost all virtual workers I've come across, both domestic and overseas, are much more interested in full-time positions than part-time ones.

The following are the primary roles that we'll be discussing throughout the book. All of these are roles that both online entrepreneurs and more traditional brick-and-mortar business owners can use when marketing and growing their businesses in today's economy.

- general virtual assistant (GVA)
- web developer
- graphic designer
- SEO (search engine optimization)/Internet marketing VA
- content writer
- video editor
- app developer

1. General Virtual Assistant (GVA)

As I've mentioned already, I'm a firm believer that every entrepreneur needs a GVA. Even if you already have a personal assistant, I recommend using a general virtual assistant as well. Not only are GVAs extremely affordable at a starting rate of around $3.50 per hour—which means they can do the lower level online work you've been giving to your personal assistant—but they're also a great way to get accustomed to the idea of virtual staffing. Trust me, it's not as scary as you think.

Pay Scale: $500 to $900 per month

Examples of Typical Duties

- Research keywords and topics.
- Maintain social media and post status updates.
- Manage your calendar, including travel and daily meetings.
- Upload blog posts and help with publishing schedules.
- Make small purchases, equipped with a prepaid credit card.
- Create and manage reports for website sales and product shipping.
- Check in with other team members, almost like a project manager. (We'll discuss this role a little later on.)

2. Web Developer

These virtual workers are incredibly skilled and typically self-taught. They can create every type of website from basic brochure-style pages to fully functional e-commerce sites.

Consider the web developer VA as a digital contractor who keeps your web presence relevant, attractive, and functional. Without a solid web developer, you'll soon find yourself with a site that becomes stale and lacks the content you need to gain higher rankings. However, keep in mind that a web developer is not responsible for designing your website. The developer's job is to bring your site to life with the proper coding and to maintain its functionality.

Pay Scale: $600 to $1,500 per month

Examples of Typical Duties

- Install and customize blog and website themes.
- Install shopping cart and "buy now" buttons.
- Create e-commerce sites.
- Create membership sites.
- Maintain backups and make sure software and plug-ins are all up to date.
- Work with PHP and other scary programming languages.

Don't worry if you don't understand some of the terms above. You don't have to understand the terminology to benefit from a web developer's skills—trust me, I know!

3. Graphic Designer

Not to be confused with your web developer, your graphic designer VA will be in charge of creating customized graphics for both offline and online marketing.

Pay Scale: $600 to $1,500 per month

Examples of Typical Duties

- Create logos and business cards.
- Design product images and retail packaging.
- Make 3-D images for video.
- Customize web icons and buttons.
- Design original websites and create new concepts.

4. SEO (Search Engine Optimization)/Internet Marketing VA

The world of SEO is a rapidly changing environment. That

means that only those professionals who stay plugged into what's going on can offer lasting results to their clients and employees. What does that mean in plain English? It means that what may have worked last year will probably be less effective or not work at all today.

For example, on April 24, 2012, Google introduced Penguin, an algorithm update that was designed to decrease the rankings of websites that violated Google's Webmaster Guidelines by using duplicate content, keyword stuffing, and other "black-hat" techniques to gain higher rankings.

Perhaps your SEO strategy never involved these kinds of tactics—but even if it didn't, there are constant changes to search-engine algorithms that will affect your ranking. This is why it's essential for you to partner with an SEO VA who can implement the most current strategies.

This virtual assistant will help you optimize your online content, which we'll discuss at great length in Section 6. Since the world of SEO changes so quickly, it's important to make sure your SEO VA is consistently educating himself or herself to stay up to date with any changes that will affect your website's ranking.

Pay Scale: $600 to $1,000 per month

Examples of Typical Duties

- Optimize page titles, meta descriptions, and keywords.
- Interlink content throughout your site.
- Perform off-site SEO tactics like link building and social bookmarking.
- Research keywords by searching for and making

regular lists of common industry search terms, helping you to focus more on your content creation.

- Maintain content across all online properties.

5. Content Writer

Your content writer is a person who loves to read and write and is good at both. It's quite easy to find someone overseas who is directly out of college with a degree in Mass Communications, Hotel and Restaurant Management, or Nursing. These degrees reflect the fact that they studied in English and have a good command of the language. However, be selective of the pieces of content you choose to outsource. I recommend that you create yourself any content that will have your name attached to it.

Pay Scale: $400 to $700 per month

Examples of Typical Duties

- Write 500- to 1,200-word blog posts.
- Create descriptions of podcasts (also known as "show notes").
- Write press releases.
- Research, outline, and write e-books and whitepapers.
- Write website content. However, I suggest that you never outsource the writing of your "About" page. The owner of the blog or business should always write this page.
- Read through articles and books you recommend to come up with similar content ideas.

- Upload articles to blogs. Not all writers will be able to do this initially, but it is an easy skill you can train your writer to do, particularly if your site runs on an easy-to-use platform like WordPress.

6. Video Editor

Due to the increasing popularity of online video marketing, I've seen a huge spike in demand for VAs who have post-production skills and are familiar with the various video marketing platforms out there. If you're not using video in your current marketing strategy, consider the following statistics specific to YouTube, keeping in mind that there are also plenty of other video sharing sites online.

- YouTube receives more than one billion unique users each month.
- More than four billion hours of video are watched on YouTube each month. It's like eating a potato chip—once you start, it's impossible to have just one!
- Seventy-two hours of video are uploaded to YouTube every minute.

Now I know many late adopters might consider YouTube to be that place where people go to escape reality by watching dancing cats and cute babies. While that's still true, people are also going to YouTube to be educated. They're searching for everything from "how to fix a flat tire" to "which camera should I buy?"

Don't worry—you don't need a film degree or expensive

equipment to produce high-quality videos that are engaging. In fact, the camera built into your smartphone can produce incredible footage that, if properly edited, could start driving targeted traffic to your website, which could lead to your next client or your next spike in sales.

A video editor VA can combine your raw footage with audio effects, video effects, and processing effects (similar to, but a little more complex than the Instagram filters you might use to make your iPhone photos look better) to produce a high-quality video that will leave you saying, "Did I really shoot that on my phone?"

For an example of the type of videos you can create with a simple iPhone 5 and a video editor VA, visit **ChrisDucker.com/SuperVAMyth**

With video editor VAs, there is a big difference in pay scales based on experience level and the quantity of effects and animation you want.

Pay Scale: $800 to $2,000 per month

Examples of Typical Duties

- Splice and edit raw video files.
- Integrate different clips and transitions to keep your audience entertained.
- Add music and other audio effects, such as zingers.
- Incorporate special effects, such as animated text. This is only necessary if it helps enhance your story or move it along. Using effects just for the heck of it will only serve as a distraction.

- Upload videos. Once edited and approved, your editor can make sure your video is properly uploaded to YouTube and other video-sharing sites.

7. App Developer

The world of mobile apps contains two schools of thought. Some believe mobile apps are just a trend that will one day become a thing of the past. Others see mobile apps as the future of mobile web browsing and even business in general.

Which is correct? As of right now, we don't know. But one thing's for sure—mobile app creation, marketing, and purchasing are all on the rise. This means that business owners must ask themselves if they want to participate and strike while the consumer buzz is hot or stick to traditional methods of interaction.

Just as for video editing, there are plenty of free tools online that allow users to create an app for next to nothing or even for free. However, I would caution you against pursuing free tools, especially when it comes to creating a user experience for your brand.

Pay Scale: $1,000 to $2,500 per month. Please note that this particular salary rate is changing at a rapid pace and is best set as a per-project payment rather than an hourly or monthly one.

Examples of Typical Duties

- Create initial design and layout options for the app.
- Build an app wireframe to show how the app will work.

- Program in various languages such as JavaScript, PHP, jQuery, Node.js, MySQL, and many more.
- Test app on various devices, such as iOS, Android, and BlackBerry, to confirm compatibility.
- Submit the app and manage it through the iTunes Store and other directories.

Keep in mind that these are just the main roles virtual staff members can fill. You'll also find that more clerical work, such as basic bookkeeping, is also being outsourced on a regular basis—and has been for more than two decades already. The bottom line is that as long as you can identify the tasks within the role and as long as the work can be done via a computer connected to the Internet, there's someone out there who can do it.

Now that you understand the importance of defining roles and have seen the different types of VAs that are available, it's time to search for potential candidates. Before we begin, let me give you a few pieces of advice on the hunting, hiring, and firing (ouch!) processes.

- **Hiring a VA is a process.** You're looking for a good fit—not the perfect fit. Don't settle on anyone, but also understand that the only way to truly know if someone will work out is to give him or her a chance. This whole thing is a learning process that will get easier for you as time goes on.
- **Listen to your gut.** If someone looks great on paper but there's a little buzzer going off in your head that's telling you to pass, don't hire that person. Simple, right?

- **Pay attention to response time.** If you're going back and forth with a potential VA and you're not happy with his or her response time—or if the candidate continues to miss specific questions in your e-mails—then expect the same type of interaction in your day-to-day workflow. Then ask yourself, "Can I live with this?"

As long as you implement the hiring practices I'm about to show you, you'll greatly increase your chances of successfully finding the right candidate.

CASE STUDY #1

Todd Beuckens, Online Teacher
Elllo

When most people consider starting an online business, it's usually to escape an unfulfilling job or to earn an extra living on the side—but that wasn't the case with Todd Beuckens. As a teacher based in Asia, Todd's passion for education inspired him to create Elllo.org, an e-learning site designed to give students and teachers the resources they need to become better educated at no charge. With more than ten years of teaching experience, Todd thoroughly understood the needs of both students and teachers. This allowed him to create the kind of content he felt was scarce online—or anywhere, for that matter.

To monetize (meaning make money directly from his website), Todd used Google AdSense and sold digital products and a few online classes. For five long years, Todd was strapped for cash. Every piece of his business, from coding his website to creating custom graphics, was his responsibility. It wasn't until he came upon a coding problem he couldn't solve that he decided to seek outside help. When he did so, Todd realized that it's infinitely more efficient to hire an extra hand than to try to teach yourself specialized skills.

After this epiphany, Todd made himself an interesting promise. Despite his passion for his teaching job, he resolved to quit the moment he had made enough income to replace his salary and to live the coveted lifestyle of a digital entrepreneur, traveling extensively and visiting exotic beaches.

But surprisingly, after eight months of soaking up the sun and living what he thought was "the dream," Todd was miserable. He realized just how much he missed teaching and his community of colleagues. Todd realized he wanted to return to teaching, but he wasn't willing to close up shop on his website or to go back to driving himself into the ground by teaching full-time while running his online business as a one-man show. He needed to find a healthy balance.

Why Virtual Staffing?

By returning to a teaching position, Todd could leverage his salary to outsource work for his online business while continuing to do the work he loved. Shortly after making this decision, Todd transitioned into professional outsourcing and now only does about 20 percent of the work he did previously in his Internet business while also working as a full-time teacher.

Todd often recalls a particular story to reiterate the power and efficiency of a workforce made up of VAs. Years ago, Todd worked in publishing and was asked to produce a series of books. He was paid $10,000 to create just one of the titles. The book contained fourteen educational lessons and was compiled by a team consisting of a co-author, designer, editor, and sales staff. From concept to distribution, the book took two years to complete and is still available for purchase today.

Compare that to a website that Todd recently created to help people learn Spanish. It's a free platform that consists of more than 300 videos of Spanish speakers from twelve different countries and various quizzes to help challenge the learner. However, the site's most impressive feature is that it was created using VAs who do not speak Spanish. The site took less than three months to complete and will be distributed in print and mobile versions as well.

Thanks to Todd's VAs, the site was created in a language he does not speak, for a fraction of the cost it would have otherwise taken to complete just the website alone, without the print or mobile iterations.

Todd's Hurdles

The biggest hurdle Todd faced was a mental block concerning the risks of owning a small business. Questions like, "Why would someone want to work for a small-time operation?" and "What if I get ripped off?" were constantly in the back of his mind.

These two questions were quickly answered once Todd took the plunge. He learned that most independent contractors and VAs prefer working for smaller businesses because they receive better treatment. Todd realized that having virtual staff was not only personally liberating, but also that most VAs are hardworking people who enjoy being a part of something that's constantly growing and improving.

Todd's Best Practices

- **Work with multiple VAs instead of hiring one full-time VA.** Instead of hiring one full-time VA to complete a project, Todd prefers working with multiple VAs who each handle a small set of tasks for a couple hours a week until a project is completed. He's also found that some VAs would rather collaborate with multiple employers for a few hours each week than hitch their carts to just one person or project. For example, let's say Todd needs 500 quizzes created for one of his teaching sites. Instead of putting all of his eggs in one basket with a single assistant, he'll hire a group of VAs so he can determine who is best suited for the job, then assign the quizzes to an equal number of VAs after dismissing those that don't quite fit the bill and boosting the hours (and workload, obviously) of those who are hitting the mark. This allows him to keep moving forward without having to begin the hiring process all over again and rewards those virtual workers who show a better fit with his plans.

- **Look for freelancers or VAs with no reviews.** Everyone needs a chance to get started, and this strategy can result in a win-win situation if executed correctly. Todd will contact these newbies, give them the rundown of his business, and offer them positions as VAs. Some of his best hires are still with him today and were found using this exact strategy.

- **Be a nice guy.** It's a simple strategy that works well. The difference between productive virtual workers who produce amazing work over a long period of time and those who dwindle away into the virtual wilderness lies in how you treat them.

Todd's Tools of the Trade

Here are the top tools Todd uses when working with his virtual staff:

- **Screencast** (Screencast.com): Step-by-step instruction on creating training content exactly the way you want it to be consumed by your VA.
- **Dropbox** (Dropbox.com): A document-sharing program that keeps everyone on the same page.

> Individual folders can be shared with different team members.
> - **Skype** (Skype.com): The best means of communicating face-to-face with your global staff.
>
> Todd's ability to communicate clearly with his VAs, to understand what they are all about, and to see how they like to work with their bosses has allowed him to maximize the output of his virtual workers. Knowing whether each worker wants to be part-time or full-time as well as what start and end times everyone prefers to work are also keys to his ongoing success.

Finding the Right Virtual Staff

There are a wide range of platforms and options to connect you with VAs for your business, each with its pros and cons. Ultimately, you'll have to choose the direction to go in, but here's my honest opinion on each option.

1. Outsourcing Companies

Staffing companies allow you to rent employees from them to perform the various tasks you need completed. I can't think of a good reason why anyone would want to take this route. Allow me to explain why.

Things to Consider

- These services are expensive because the outsourcing companies profit by marking up the cost of each VA's work.
- The VAs are not part of your team—they're paid by the outsourcing company and not by you.

- There's little opportunity to create loyalty and trust because the worker is employed by the outsourcing company and not directly by you.
- If the outsourcing company goes out of business, all of your help will be lost overnight.

2. Job-Posting Sites

Elance.com, oDesk.com, and Craigslist.org all fall into this category. Job-posting sites are the best way to find virtual workers to whom you can outsource your project-based tasks. The way that you use these sites is quite simple:

1. Post a task or project that needs to be completed.
2. Set a price you're willing to pay.
3. Get offers from freelancers.
4. Award a freelancer the job.
5. Set project milestones and begin!

Things to Consider

- You'll be able to quickly find people to complete individual projects.
- You can see past reviews to get an idea of the worker's performance.
- You are one of many clients each person is working with, and the workers understand that you may only work with them on just one project (although you do have the ability to work with them again if you like them). This can make it difficult to establish a good working relationship with a set routine.

- Rather than trying to make one full-time employer or two or three part-time employers happy, these types of VAs get paid more when they turn out higher volumes of work. As a result, the quality of the work may suffer.

3. Freelancer Marketplace Sites

The recent economic downturn combined with the popularity of job-posting sites has inspired many people to venture out on their own and create "VA for hire" services. These people are skilled freelancers with specific skills who classify themselves as entrepreneurs rather than VAs—and they are particularly popular in the United States, the United Kingdom, and Australia. Check out sites like Freelancer.com, Guru.com, and Fiverr.com to find an abundance of such freelancers.

Typically, you can expect to pay more for individual tasks or blocks of time via these types of sites in comparison with job-posting sites.

Things to Consider

- If you're a first-time outsourcer, get started by trying things out by simply assigning a quick and simple-to-complete task. These types of freelancers are accustomed to selling their own services and will take the time to walk you through what they do.
- These freelancers will want to establish ongoing relationships with you.
- These freelancers are highly skilled, and they are

also entrepreneurs, which means they charge premium prices for their services.

- Since you're working with one person and someone with an entrepreneurial mindset, you may find that he or she is more opinionated and less flexible than someone found on a job-posting website, for example.

4. VA Recruiting Services

A firm providing you with a pool of potential VAs is a relatively new concept that has only been around for the last few years. In the interest of full disclosure, I should note that I own such a company, VirtualStaffFinder.com (focusing on the GVA role discussed above). To find a VA using this method, you sign up for the recruiting service, submit a job description, and then sit back and relax. You can focus on running your company while the recruiting team does the interviewing, background checks, testing, and additional screening needed to create a finalized list of candidates. Then you'll interview the candidates, typically via Skype, and hire the one whom you are confident you can get to work with right away.

Things to Consider

- VA recruiting services are a simple and efficient way to find a VA because you don't have to do any of the legwork.
- You'll benefit from the experience of job-placement professionals who handle these types of recruiting situations daily.

45

- The VA becomes your direct employee and therefore a part of your team—trained and managed directly by you, unlike some freelance workers you will find on job-posting sites, who will probably want to continue to work with other clients.

- Recruiting services have an excellent hit-to-miss ratio. They are an effective way to find the right people for the roles you're looking to fill and avoid hiring the wrong people.

• • •

While the above methods are the heavy hitters, they aren't the only means out there for finding good quality VAs—if you're willing to do a little extra work, you could also try using social media to find your VA. After a poor first experience with outsourcing, janitor-turned-entrepreneur David Risley turned to Twitter to find his next VA, and he loves the simplicity of the microblogging site.

In closing this subject, I suggest that whenever possible, you chat—and ideally video chat—with the person you're hiring via a service like Skype or Google Hangouts. This will give you the opportunity to see, or at least hear, your potential VA and understand his or her personality a little more. This might not be needed all the time; I doubt I'd be concerned with personality if someone were just designing a logo for me, for example. But in some cases this "face-to-face" conversation might turn out to be the difference between hiring and not hiring someone for the job.

The 10 Elements of a Good Job Description

I can't stress this enough: Hiring the right people begins with defining the roles your business needs.

Once the roles are defined, the next step is to create a solid job description that will help you attract the right candidates if you're using a job-posting site and will serve as a guide through the interview process if you use a recruiting service. Putting in the time and effort to create a really strong job description will enable you to find the right people to work in your business.

Here are the ten elements a good job description should have:

1. Job Title

The title should clearly reflect the role. Avoid gimmicky or misleading titles.

Here are a few examples of particularly good job titles I've seen recently:

- Part-Time Data Entry VA Needed for Growing Tour Company
- Graphic Designer Needed for Children's Kindle Project
- Web Developer Needed for E-mail Newsletter Template Design
- Virtual Assistant Needed to Support CEO on Daily To-Do List Items

2. Type of Position

Note whether the job is project based, part time, or full time.

3. Working Time Zone

In which time zone are you working and in which time zone do you require your VA(s) to be working? This allows candidates to see at a quick glance what your working structure will be like together.

4. Skills

What particular skills will this role require? Be extremely specific here.

5. Daily Reporting and Accountability

In order to avoid confusion or miscommunication, you should have your team members give a quick report at the end of each day summarizing what they worked on and any progress or problems. This can be done through a simple e-mail or by updating a shared document via a file-sharing service like Google Drive or Dropbox. It's a good idea to note your expectations of daily reporting in a job description.

6. Proposed Compensation

This is what are you willing to pay. You can specify a maximum number of hours per month for part-time workers or maximum monthly pay for full-time VAs. Be sure to offer what you feel the VA is genuinely worth.

7. Daily Work Description

Write a concise description of the duties and responsibilities for this particular role. The more detailed it is, the better.

This might include

- key skills required on a day-to-day basis
- daily tasks to be performed
- experience required in using certain tools, software, and systems
- hardware requirements, such as a webcam or scanner

8. Weekly Work Description

If applicable, list the revolving weekly tasks the person in this role should expect to perform for you.

9. Quarterly Tasks

List work that will not need to be done daily or weekly but will need to be completed on a quarterly basis, such as updating spreadsheets, attending brainstorming sessions, and making suggestions on how to improve your systems and processes.

10. Potentially Harder Tasks and Skills

This is an opportunity to highlight the more difficult skills you're looking for. It's important to ask your VA how he or she is continuing to enhance these skills. Be careful here, though—you don't want to scare the VA away!

No matter where you found them, once you've solidified your job description and the applicants have started to present themselves, the next step is to chat with the people who look the most exciting on paper.

This is a job description that we received recently from a Virtual Staff Finder client. You'll see how simply it's laid out while still being quite detailed. This is how organized you need to be if you want to do this thing right from the outset.

Job Title	General VA
Position Type	Full-Time
Time Zone	Happy to have them work their normal workday hours.
Daily Reporting	Just a simple bullet-point e-mail at the end of each day is fine.
Proposed Compensation	Starting at $550 per month with a review at 12 months.
Elaborate on Tasks and Skills	**General** eye for detail excellent English reading and writing ability to clearly follow instructions high level of organization and ability to prioritize self-management and initiative **Daily Tasks** Clean up new database entries from the last 24 hours. Check e-mails and reply to all e-mails that you can do. Check Facebook personal messages. Accept new Facebook friends and categorize by list. Send a personal e-mail to everyone who joins client database, so we can tag.

Elaborate on Tasks and Skills (CONTINUED)	Send e-mails to new members for photos and to add them to the Facebook group. Schedule social media updates in HootSuite.

Weekly Tasks

Call everyone who has stopped receiving e-mails to get new e-mail addresses.

Ensure that your computer is backed up and all files are in more than one place.

Add new posts on our blogs.

Load new member photos in template and upload files to Dropbox.

Comment on other related YouTube channels.

Quarterly Tasks

Transcribe any new YouTube videos and upload transcription.

Create spreadsheets of contact data from websites.

Ongoing/Revolving Tasks

Clean up old database: filter spam, unsubscribes, etc.

Create playlists for all current YouTube videos.

Follow up on undeliverable mail: call people to get correct addresses and update in database.

Online research: sourcing gifts, restaurants, etc.

Visit **VirtualFreedomBook.com/Reader** to download a job description template as well as a fully completed GVA job description for ideas and inspiration.

CASE STUDY #2

Tom Libelt, Online Service Provider
Libelty SEO

Although originally from Poland, Tom Libelt spent most of his childhood in Polish communities in Chicago and New York. An early entrepreneur, Tom co-owned a clothing/record store when he was just sixteen years old. Though it didn't bring in the big bucks, it did whet his appetite for business.

His journey into digital entrepreneurship began when he started creating AdSense sites. It only took him a couple of weeks to figure out the basics of web design before he was up and running. That's when the real work began.

Tom quickly found himself swamped with the tasks involved in keeping such an operation afloat. Between keyword research, backlinking, and writing 500-word articles on random topics like train models and Christmas lights, Tom's days quickly turned into a nonstop grind. His schedule was seriously threatening his sanity and causing him to resent his work. Unable to keep working at such a demanding pace, he realized LibeltySEO.com needed help.

Why Virtual Staffing?

While researching solutions for his productivity problem, Tom remembered a business forum that related the details of outsourcing and VA use. One participant in particular kept raving about his staff in the Philippines—how great they were to work with and how they were running his empire while he had all the time in the world. This piqued Tom's interest. He realized that if he could reclaim even a fraction of his time, it would make a huge impact in the way his business functioned.

Tom's Hurdles

When starting out, Tom had no idea what type of average salary a VA should receive. Though he remembers seriously low-balling offers to his potential VAs, he surprisingly still attracted some interest.

His first few hires produced questionable work at best, but Tom was so tired and burnt out from doing everything himself that he was just happy to have someone—anyone—showing interest in collaborating with him. He figured he could always go back and edit their work.

Tom hired three people during the first three months of his new venture and quickly realized that outsourcing can actually create *more* work if a business owner isn't careful. In addition to his managerial position, Tom now had to edit and post all of the work his VAs did. And that's when the next obstacle surfaced—turnover.

As soon as a VA began working with Tom and producing content, it only took a couple weeks before he or she began missing deadlines or going completely AWOL. Not only was this pattern frustrating, but also the effort it took to replace the VAs was incredibly time consuming.

The initial plan looked something like this:

- Tom supplies topics to be written about.
- VAs write about topic and then turn it into Tom.
- Tom posts the content on his site.

But here's what really happened:

- Tom supplied topics to be written about.
- VAs wrote only a few of them and then didn't respond for days.
- Tom spent an enormous amount of time editing the VAs' work.
- Tom posted the content on his site long after his expected post dates.

It took three years and many bad hires for Tom to finally find a team he can trust. However, time and lessons allowed Tom to build two companies—an SEO company and a publishing company—that he now runs with VAs he can depend on.

Tom's Best Practices

Tom has certainly experienced his fair share of lessons when it comes to virtual staffing. Here are a few of his best tips:

- **Bad hires are part of the learning process.** You won't always be able to identify a bad hire when interviewing, so don't beat yourself up. Some people will oversell the fact that they have college degrees, which can easily sway your decision. Make sure the candidate is who you're looking for in terms of skill sets and values before hiring.

- **Use your best VA to help interview potential candidates.** The best way to identify good potential candidates is to use one of your star employees or someone from the same country as your VA to first qualify the candidate over the phone. This doesn't mean you'll automatically hire anyone the VA likes or refers, but it will help to increase your odds of getting quality new hires. You can also check feedback from other business owners, if you're hiring via a job-posting website.

- **Keep your communication clear and simple.** Clarity is key when outsourcing—and clarity equals simplicity. The goals and expectations you have for your VA should be easily understandable and measurable. This allows both of you to have a fair way to measure performance. Once you've established measurable goals and expectations, make sure you regularly track the VA's progress. Tom does this through monthly meetings via Skype and yearly evaluations of his staff, which is when he decides if they deserve a salary increase.

Tom's Tools of the Trade

Here are the top three tools Tom uses when working with his virtual staff:

- **Basecamp** (Basecamp.com): Enables you to keep track and stay on top of multiple projects with several team members cross-working.
- **Skype** (Skype.com): The perfect tool for communicating face-to-face with your global staff. Tom particularly likes the screen-sharing option.
- **Jing** (Techsmith.com/Jing): An online program that allows for simultaneous screen captures and audio and video recording. This program makes your instructions and goals simple and clear. It's a real favorite with virtual trainers.

As Tom discovered, the odd bad hire was ultimately a part of the learning curve he needed to maneuver in order to take things to the next level. Through a combination of location research via Google and using his current staff to find new team members, Tom can now effectively run his companies entirely with the help of his VAs.

The Interview Process
(and the 10 Questions You Should Ask)

I can tell you from my own experience in working with thousands of virtual assistants that the increased demand for virtual staff has increased cost and invited opportunity-seekers, i.e. people who don't really possess the skills you're looking for but figure they'll just pick them up while on the job. Unfortunately, that's the way things go when demand increases in any field—but this shouldn't alarm you. There are a lot of great VAs out there, and you'll have no problem connecting with one and sniffing out any imposters by following this interviewing process.

Before I continue, here's a little tip to remember about interviews: The interview process begins from the first point of interaction and continues on through to the beginning of employment. From e-mail correspondence to building rapport with small talk, every interaction should be considered a part of the interview process. All of these interactions are painting a picture of the type of person who will be impacting you and your business.

Even when you think you've found the perfect match, you should continue to ask yourself from time to time if the person is still right for the role. Companies can outgrow employees and even founders from time to time, so be aware of that.

Successful online entrepreneur Ryan Lee has a number of VAs, all of whom he has hired personally to help grow his very virtual business. (His office is his local Starbucks!) He recognizes that there is a big difference between being the employee and the employer, and when hiring virtual staff, he pays very close attention to the interviews as the beginning of the entire virtual management process.

As a side comment here, it's also a good idea to remember that this goes both ways. Your virtual staff members are continuously looking to you to determine whether or not you are the type of person they want to continue working with. Keep that in mind, too.

FINDING AND HIRING YOUR VIRTUAL STAFF

The 3 Components of a Good Hire

In my view, a good hire should have the following qualities:

1. **Skills**: First and foremost, the candidate should have the necessary skills you're looking for.

2. **Growth potential**: The candidate should show evidence that she or he is continually developing his or her skills. That means a potential VA should be able to reference some sort of training taken in the last twelve months, whether provided by an employer or sought out by the VA himself or herself (something that really stands out to me as an employer).

3. **Personality**: The candidate's personality should mesh well with yours and with the overall vibe of your organization. It does no good to have talented people with whom you and your other employees cannot stand to interact.

Failing to have all three of these qualities will eventually lead to a huge bite in your bottom...line. (See what I did there? That may just be the only pun in the entire book, but I couldn't resist!)

So how do you make sure these qualities are present? Great question. And my answer is to ask potential VAs some specific questions of your own.

Here are the ten questions that I continually use to help me secure good hires. You'd be wise to ask the same questions of your VA candidates.

1. **Why did you leave your last job—or why do you want to leave your current job?** This question allows you to see why your VA could potentially be leaving your organization one day.

2. **What did you like about your last job?** This will let you know how the VA works best and what motivates him or her.

3. **What do you know about me and my organization?** If you've given candidates your website and name, this is a good opportunity to see if they've done their homework on you. If you haven't given them your website, perhaps they've been aggressive enough to Google you and find out about you anyway, which is a great quality.

4. **What skills do you have that make you a perfect fit for this role?** Look at the bullet points in your job description and see if the candidate offers specific comments that reflect knowledge of what you're looking for in a VA.

5. **Do you have any other skills that were not on the job description that might be useful to me and my organization?** Your VA may have other skills that could enhance the role you're looking to fill. Though this doesn't happen as often as we might like, it's obviously a bonus when it does occur.

6. **Tell me about yourself. What do you like to do outside of work?** This question is purely

meant to build rapport. VAs view their bosses—in this case, you—as an authority figure, but they also want to know that you view them as human beings. Their answers will also give you a little insight into their personalities.

7. **What have you done in the last twelve months to improve your skills?** Back to business! Candidates should have had some sort of training in the last twelve months. I would recommend taking this question one step further and asking when and where the training took place.

8. **How long would you expect to work for me if you got the job?** The virtual way of working can sometimes be on and off for the virtual worker, so giving him or her a sense of security based on performance can buy instant loyalty. I typically tell the people I hire, "As long as you continue to do good work, you'll have a job with me for as long as I'm in business." I genuinely mean that, and it also goes a long way in establishing a sense of loyalty in my workers—which helps to bring out their best.

9. **If I was to hire you today, what would make you an asset to my company?** This is a very open-ended question that may feel like a repeat of early questions, but I look at it as the candidate's chance to wrap everything up and sell me on why I should hire him or her. So just sit back, don't say a word, and see how the candidate responds.

10. **What do you expect to get paid for this role/ project/job?** Getting the money topic out into the open and onto the table at the end of the call is absolutely necessary for you to figure out whether or not you can afford the particular candidate. If your budget is close to his or her expected compensation figure, this is when you can negotiate.

Although a lot of virtual bosses like the idea of sending these types of questions via e-mail or some other type of on-line portal, such as on the job-posting websites themselves, I sincerely suggest doing interviews in person.

With the Internet and software such as Skype and Google Hangouts at your disposal, in my mind you're mad to not connect face-to-face (virtually, that is) when making such an incredibly important businesses decision.

Once you've decided on a candidate and you're ready to hire, be sure to spend some time looking into the candidate's work history and speak to one or two of their past employers, if possible.

Confidentiality and Contracts

My advice on handling confidentiality and putting things like contracts and nondisclosure agreements in place follows this brief disclaimer: Keep in mind that I am not a lawyer in your city, state, or country. For that matter, I'm not a lawyer anywhere! If you're in doubt, speak with a local expert in these matters.

The following information comes from personal experience collated together with the feedback I've collected from clients and others who have and continue to work with virtual staff members.

Although every situation is different, contracts are great for outlining job descriptions and compensation. If you're keeping things closer to home and working with a domestic-based VA, your contract is obviously going to be a lot more watertight. Though it's highly unlikely that you'll have a disagreement that will require legal action, if you do and you're working with overseas VAs, the agreement you have in place simply won't hold up in a court.

The real secret to protecting yourself from any potential confidentiality issues is to use common sense when working with your virtual staff, especially at the beginning of your relationship.

Here are a few tips that I frequently suggest people take on board:

- Consider using a password protector like LastPass (Lastpass.com).
- Never share any access to online banking or credit card accounts.
- If you want your VA to handle PayPal payments and similar tasks, create a separate account from the one that you receive funds into and simply transfer funds to the second account for the VA to use.
- Be sure that you back up any CRM (customer relationship management) content or databases that contain client information on a regular basis. Of course, you can also have your VA do this for you.

NDAs (Nondisclosure Agreements)

NDAs are basically not worth the paper they are printed on. However, like a VA job contract, they are good for setting ground rules and expectations of what your employee can and cannot discuss outside of your working relationship.

Acting a little like a security blanket, an NDA is typically shorter than a contract—and your VA will most likely actually read the entire document from beginning to end. I also feel like the term "nondisclosure agreement" sounds a little scarier than a simple "contract," so team members are more likely to pay attention and stick to the NDA's contents.

In closing on this subject, you shouldn't be any more or less concerned about confidentiality with a virtual employee than you would be with someone employed in your local office. Bad apples are just that; they do exist, but as long as you pay attention to your gut instinct, you'll be just fine. My gut rarely lets me down.

Once all these steps are in place and you're ready to start working with your new virtual employee, there's one topic we need to discuss to make sure you avoid a major mistake that a lot of entrepreneurs plough into: training—or rather, the lack of it.

SECTION TWO

Training Your Virtual Staff

In 2007, Tim Ferriss released his book *The 4-Hour Workweek: Escape 9–5, Live Anywhere, and Join the New Rich.* Overnight, the entrepreneurial world dove into a virtual assistant frenzy.

A lot of people, myself included, were already using VAs on a small scale at the time—but Tim's book gave the virtual working world a spotlight within the entrepreneurial ecosystem and created a tidal wave of demand. Thanks, Tim!

At the time, I was entrenched in building my call center company and consulting with small- to medium-size organizations about implementing new VA programs or expanding existing ones. So when Tim's book hit number one on *The New York Times* bestsellers list, I braced myself for that tidal wave to come crashing down.

My organization was flooded with inquiries from all types of business owners and entrepreneurs who wanted to get their hands on what they believed to be the new silver bullet of the small business world. But as they soon discovered, there's more to this game than simply hiring a VA.

We'll break down the training part of the virtual freedom process by exploring the following topics:

- why the biggest problem when training virtual staff can be yourself
- how you can really get to know your VAs
- the VA Training Trifecta
- best practices to follow when training your virtual staff
- why throwing your VA a curveball is sometimes a good thing
- the VA Success Equation and what it means to your overall success

This section contains both strategic and tactical approaches to training virtual workers. I'll do my best to simplify the topic as much as possible because it is an area where a lot of people trip up. As long as you keep in mind that this is a learning process for both you and your VA—one that takes continual improvement and testing—you'll do just fine.

The Biggest Problem with Training Virtual Workers: You!

Here's a little secret no one tells you: The first person you'll need to train when working with virtual staff is yourself. That's right. You. You're the one in charge. You're the one with the vision. You're the one who's battling superhero syndrome—remember?

The biggest and most surprising problem I see in current VA training isn't improper training or overtraining, but rather a complete lack of training. Too many people think their VA comes ready to use "out of the box." But your VA is a human being, not a software plugin.

Sorry, but there's no magic pill to pop here. It's going to

take some good old-fashioned digital elbow grease to get things moving. Let's begin by discussing three important elements that will set you on the right path, the first two of which we've already discussed a little.

1. Defining the Role

Before you can begin training a VA, you must define the role.

Small Business Trends CEO and publisher Anita Campbell knows exactly where I'm coming from on the concept of hiring for the role, not the task. She strongly believes that tasks should be grouped and delegated to VAs based on their functional expertise. In other words, SEO tasks should only be given to VAs who focus on providing SEO services as their main role.

So start off by asking yourself a few questions, such as

- What are the core responsibilities of the role the VA will fill?
- What skills or traits does he or she need to properly fulfill it?
- How will you measure success within this role?

It's also helpful to consider who else on your team will be interacting with the VA and then find a person who will be a good match.

Even if you're just starting with a GVA, this exercise will help you identify your needs, which should be the primary drive behind your decision-making process. Refer back to your 3 Lists to Freedom that we discussed in the opening of the book. This is a great tool that will help you identify the roles you'll need to create.

2. Setting Expectations

Setting expectations between you and your VA is the cornerstone to successful virtual staffing. But remember, this is a two-way street. Your VA will also be counting on you to hold up your end of the deal.

Here are some questions to consider:

- When will you pay: weekly, biweekly, monthly, or when a project is completed? We'll go more into this subject in Section 3 of the book.
- How much will you pay?
- How will you track progress?
- What kind of response times do you expect for e-mail communications between you and your VA?
- What will you do if the work performed does not meet your standards?

3. Training, Not Assuming

Would you get mad at your calculator if you accidentally pressed the number two instead of five? Of course not... at least I hope not! The same principle applies when you're communicating with virtual staff members. One of the greatest mistakes you can make as a leader is to assume your staff knows what you meant to say or what you should have said.

This is why the number-one rule to successfully harnessing the power of your virtual staff is never to assume anything—ever. That doesn't mean your VA lacks common sense or is unable to connect the dots. What it means is that you need to be clear and concise. Don't expect your VA to be a mind reader or to do something different than what you asked of him or her.

One of my first virtual assistant consulting clients owned a medium-size company that was having trouble hiring the right person. They had already fired their last two GVAs whom they had found via job boards, and they were about to let their current one go, so they called me in.

This new client of mine—let's just call him Mr. X—was using his GVA to perform the following tasks:

- Research competitive products online after Mr. X supplied competitor websites and industry search terms.
- Make small online purchases such as royalty-free images and books from Amazon after Mr. X supplied a $500 prepaid Visa card to limit the potential risk of overspending.
- Coordinate lunch meetings with clients via e-mail and then update Mr. X's calendar.
- Work on Mr. X's Facebook presence after Mr. X supplied a spreadsheet of regular status updates and images to upload.

I was impressed. Mr. X had obviously hired for a specific role rather than hiring someone to do a bunch of unrelated tasks. These were all tasks that would easily fall under the duties of a GVA. So far, so good.

"It seems like you've got everything well thought out," I said. "What can I help you with?"

At first, I thought he was going to say that his VA had changed security passwords or was able to hack into his online merchant account—but neither of those was the case.

"There just seems to be a lack of common sense!" he said.

Apparently, Mr. X had a new love interest, and her birthday was approaching quickly. Mr. X wanted to buy her a purse that she had lusted over when they went window-shopping the previous weekend, but he didn't have the time to drive back to the store and pick it up. Instead, he remembered the designer's name and figured this was the perfect job for his VA. However, things didn't go as planned.

Mr. X showed me the VA's response, an e-mail containing a spreadsheet with over thirty links to different purses from the designer he had requested.

"So what's the problem?" I asked.

"Chris. Where are the product images and prices? There's over thirty links here, and I have to click on every one of them to see the purse and its price. I don't have time for this. Where's the common sense?"

"Well, did you have the common sense to say you wanted images and prices to be included on the spreadsheet?" I replied.

Silence—and then Mr. X quietly answered, "No."

Lesson learned. Mr. X kept the VA and found the link to the right purse. I'm sure his lady friend ended up happy!

As for me, thankfully I wasn't only called out there to talk about purses and common sense. We ended up developing a plan to grow Mr. X's VA program in order to alleviate many of his most time-consuming tasks.

Here are two other assumptions that I've seen rear their ugly heads over and over again:

- **If a VA doesn't know how to do something, he or she will immediately ask for help.** Across the board, most VAs would rather try and figure something out themselves instead of saying, "I don't know how to do this," or, "I need help." In their eyes, asking these questions means letting you down. That's why it's important to consistently let your VA know that you welcome any questions that haven't already been addressed in training.

- **The VA will understand your definition of "a reasonable amount of time."** Here's a typical direction many VAs receive: "Please (insert task here), but don't take too much time on it. Just do your best and then move on." What's the definition of too much time? One hour? Four hours? An entire day?

Instead, try saying: "Please (insert task here), but don't take any more than two hours on it. If you've reached the end of the two hours and haven't finished, let me know and we can talk about it."

This allows you to set boundaries and check-in points so that you can see how things are progressing—and it also creates a healthy challenge for the VA. Remember that whole idea of the VA not wanting to let you down? When you give VAs time limits, you'll typically find that they finish their tasks within the established timeframes. If your VA still ends up coming back to you requesting more time, it's probably because he or she really needs it.

CASE STUDY #3

Tristan King, Location-Independent Entrepreneur
Shopify Ninjas

Tristan King loves traveling the globe and learning foreign languages—he already knows five!—but he might argue that his greatest passion is business. He started Shopify Ninjas after becoming disenchanted with his previous career as a corporate consultant who constantly climbed ladders to attain heights that didn't inspire him. Based out of Melbourne, Australia, ShopifyNinjas.com specializes in web-related services that help other business owners and entrepreneurs set up, customize, and run their e-commerce stores online.

After a short time, business was booming—and Tristan was swamped in a sea of inquiries that he couldn't keep up with on his own. It didn't take long for him to realize he needed to make the switch from working as a freelancer to becoming the head of a small team. But where could he find these extra players?

Why Virtual Staffing?

Tristan had two goals in mind when he started his business: he wanted to take a friendly, personal approach to his clients and become location-independent. He saw no reason that a physical office space would ensure quality customer service, so the choice to hire virtual staff was a no-brainer.

Tristan receives professional collaboration and pays less for his team than he would have if he had hired local workers—and his staff members have the opportunity to learn new skills for a successfully expanding business. With an overseas staff, Tristan's business is also able to offer round-the-clock services. Shopify Ninjas can run nonstop thanks to separate time zones and opposite sleeping schedules for Tristan and his staff.

Since outsourcing his business, Tristan has had no trouble justifying his choice. He recently returned from a three-month trip to South America and found that he was able to run his business just as efficiently as if he'd been at home. That kind of freedom is brought about because he doesn't have an office of employees to look over. He can also take a much more focused approach to growing his business because he is doing less technical work and more developmental work, particularly with marketing and the growth of his client base.

While Tristan certainly benefits from his virtual staff, he also recognizes the aspects of his system that benefit the whole team. He recently set up an account through lynda .com to offer his team members virtual courses and training in skill areas such as word processing, PowerPoint, and SEO. Tristan feels like he's really making a difference in his developers' professional lives by providing them with an environment where they can grow and flourish.

Tristan's Hurdles

Similar to most entrepreneurs who look for virtual workers online, Tristan initially struggled to find people who were perfectly suited for his company. When he ran ads on free local websites in Australia, he received plenty of résumés— but very few from candidates who were truly qualified.

Fortunately, with a little help from the freelancer entrepreneurship development program Location Rebel (LocationRebel.com) by Sean Ogle, Tristan learned how to be more selective and exclusive when choosing where to post job offers and find freelancers.

Tristan's Best Practices

- **Maintain constant communication.** With one developer in Sweden and one in the United States, Tristan has to maintain a constant line of communication with his staff. They e-mail regularly,

Skype often, and keep on the same page to stay up to date on tasks and projects. Communication is important in any working environment, and it is even more crucial when your team is spread throughout the world.

- **Take responsibility.** In order to develop a smooth virtual collaboration, Tristan suggests taking responsibility for your mistakes. He has found that when a project doesn't turn out correctly, it is usually his fault for not making his task descriptions clear and concise. He recommends writing clearly, using screenshots and mockups to give direction, and asking for regular feedback and understanding from team members. Taking responsibility for your staff's efforts will reflect your leadership abilities and make you a much more relatable boss and team player.

Tristan's Tools of the Trade

Here are the top three tools Tristan uses in working with his virtual staff:

- **FreshBooks** (FreshBooks.com): Great for time-tracking and invoicing when you need to charge clients or create project estimates.
- **Trello** (Trello.com): Offers project management and file storage while also allowing you to track status and receive deliverables. Best of all, it's free!
- **Skype** (Skype.com): Conduct interviews, hold catch-up calls, and receive voicemails through Skype.

Tristan's amazing focus on customer service—and the fact that he recognizes mistakes as his own nine out of ten times—have helped him to grow his company in a strategic customer-centric manner with an emphasis on continuing improvement.

While enjoying a lifestyle as an entrepreneur who is rarely in one location for any longer than it takes to start

> and finish a project, Tristan still manages to successfully operate a dynamic and fast-moving company that stays true to its focus: helping small businesses build great-looking websites.

Get to Know Your VAs

Here's the deal with training VAs: it doesn't have to be difficult—in fact, it shouldn't be—but it must be intentional. That means you need to put some thought into the various tasks you want your VA to do and then communicate how you want those tasks done.

Note that there is a difference between communicating tasks and projects (best done in writing or via video or audio recording, which we'll learn more about in a while) and giving feedback to your virtual staff. I always suggest that feedback be given verbally—for example, via services like Skype. This is to make sure nothing is lost in translation and that you can use the tone of your voice to get certain points across more easily.

Before you begin the actual training period, you'll need to get to know your new employee a little better. Because of the distance between you, you won't see them in the office every day, overhear their conversations, and see their reaction to certain situations. It's time to put together a getting-to-know-you questionnaire.

Include simple questions such as the following, along with anything more you want to find out about your new worker:

- What are the main public holidays in your country?

VIRTUAL FREEDOM

- How do you like to spend your weekends?
- What are your favorite types of movies, music, and food?
- Do you have specific work hours during which you feel you are the most productive?
- What would be the best day for us to get together on a service like Skype each week?
- What would be your preferred method of communicating with me, day to day?
- How do you see yourself helping me grow my business?

You'll see I've mixed in some personal questions with businesslike questions. This is because you want to make it clear that although you're showing interest in what they are all about, this is still a business relationship.

This activity also gives you the opportunity to tell the VA a little more about yourself— what makes you tick and how you see the business developing with their involvement—so spend some time covering that, too.

Develop Your Training Tools: The VA Training Trifecta

A lot of business owners get worried at the thought of training new staff, especially virtual staff. I'm here to tell you that it's not painful and doesn't need to be a headache.

Here is what I call the VA Training Trifecta: three ways of disseminating information in a clear, concise manner so that your virtual staff can learn quickly and effectively.

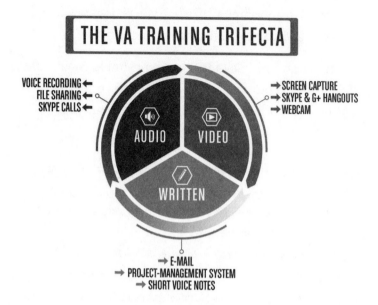

1. Written Instructions

E-mail is not dead. It's still a great tool and will probably be the primary source of communication between you and your virtual staff, along with file transfers and project-management software (which we'll go into in the next section), so it's in your best interest to learn how to write clear and concise instructions.

A few best practices include

- Use plenty of bullet points.
- Save important correspondence in a separate folder.
- Have one clear, overall objective per e-mail if possible.

- Give examples of what you're looking for via screenshots, links, and attachments.

Here's an example of how a recent simple e-mail got the job done on a project I had my VA handle, prior to opening our first co-working space here in Cebu, Philippines.

Hi Michelle:

Thanks for successfully completing your last task. You did a great job!

Now I'd like to have you help me with our new goal of collating information on co-working spaces in Asia, as I am considering opening one in the near future.

To accomplish this, I need you to do the following:

Task #1:
Do a general search on co-working spaces in Southeast Asia and make a list in a spreadsheet document. Please include the company name, the city and country they are based in, and a website address. I'm looking to have at least 10 different companies to look at.

Task #2:
Narrow this search down to the Philippines. I doubt there will be many, but please list all of them in a separate Word document, and as well as the info needed above. Include the following information, too:

Twitter ID and number of followers
Facebook page link (if available)
Name of business owner and Twitter ID if you can track it down (try using LinkedIn)

Task #3:
I'd also like for you to put together a list of five nice-looking videos that you find on YouTube, of co-working spaces in Asia. This way I can see how they look, the layout, the different things they do to make their guests and customers comfortable, etc.

Please complete the above tasks by end of work on Tuesday next week. Let me know if you have questions.

Thanks and I look forward to checking it all out!

Best,
Chris

As you can see, I thanked my VA for the work that she completed for me recently, before clearly listing the different tasks I needed done and setting a deadline.

🖱 *Download my personal Written Task Template at* **VirtualFreedomBook.com/Reader** *so you can make all of your written delegation as clear as mine above.*

---

2. Audio Recordings

If writing is not your thing, then recorded trainings will be your best bet. Simply record your message on a smartphone or laptop using software like Audacity for PC or GarageBand for Mac. Speak as if you were talking face-to-face with your VA and remember to keep each recording focused on one topic.

A few best practices include

- Be clear and concise and avoid rambling. I know that as entrepreneurs, we sometimes fall in love with the sound of our own voices—but I'm sure that's not you, right?
- Create separate recordings for separate training subjects. It's completely unfair to dump twenty to forty minutes of audio containing instructions

for multiple tasks and projects on a VA. Save the instructions in separate folders by topic in Dropbox for easy searching later on.

- Label each audio file with a title that clearly communicates the objective of the recording so that both yourself and your VA can search for and find it easily.
- Always save your recordings. They can be used to train future VAs over and over again.
- Don't forget online chat platforms like Skype— they are great live audio training tools.

3. Video Recordings

Videos are my personal favorite format to use for training new VAs. The good news is that you have a few different options here. First, you can simply record yourself to allow your VA(s) to see you personally and get a sense of how you emphasize certain instructions. This is also a strong way to build rapport.

Secondly, you can shoot screencasts, which are videos of your computer screen. This is by far my favorite training method. Screencasts have worked brilliantly for myself and for those business owners to whom I've suggested them, for the following reasons:

- The visual and audio combination leaves little room for confusion.
- You can train on your own time and not worry about syncing schedules.
- Every time you create a new video, you're adding to a vault of training material for future VAs

to learn from and reference. This is especially important if the training is focused on a repetitive task that will always need to be done in your business.

- They are actually a lot of fun and are very easy to produce!

The two platforms I recommend for PC users are Camtasia (Techsmith.com/Camtasia) and Jing (Techsmith.com/Jing). If you're using a Mac, like me, you can also use Jing; however, ScreenFlow (Telestream.net/ScreenFlow) has a little more power behind it. What I love about ScreenFlow is that I can record myself via webcam simultaneously within the screencast so my VAs can actually see my face while I'm training them.

Lastly, a live webcam training with your VA is a great way to train *and* build rapport. If you have more than one VA that you'd like to train in this manner, you can easily all hop onto a Google Hangout, so everyone can speak and be seen.

There are plenty of other options out there, so take a look around for something you feel comfortable working with. However, before you begin making a single video, I recommend checking out YouTube to see if the training you're about to create has already been made. I have personally leveraged YouTube for a lot of my VA trainings and I suggest you do the same. There are videos there that cover everything from setting up a WordPress blog for the first time to putting together a high-quality PowerPoint presentation. You've gotta love it!

CASE STUDY #4

Kyle Zimmerman, Fashion Photographer Turned Studio Owner
Kyle Zimmerman Photography

In 1985, Kyle Zimmerman—then a radical punk rocker complete with orange mohawk and a torn-up black leather jacket—started shooting hardcore rockbands and up-and-coming models for some of the top fashion agencies in the United States.

Working as a photographer in the fashion game had its perks, such as spending time in Italy, Spain, and Greece, but Kyle grew tired of having her work picked apart by editors and other fashion magazine staffers.

Fast forward to 1999: Kyle moved from San Francisco to Albuquerque, New Mexico's Nob Hill neighborhood to open up her photography studio, where she focused on shooting families and used the simple branding slogan "Life is art" to catapult her studio to one of the top three in the city.

Kyle spent years building a team; then things got tough in 2008, and she was forced to let all but one employee go—her key assistant photographer. Following this she was given a copy of MJ DeMarco's book *The Millionaire Fastlane* and got the jolt she needed to stop feeling sorry for herself and get back to work.

Why Virtual Staffing?

As things continued to be tough through 2010, Kyle started looking outside of her studio's four walls for the help she needed to continue to run her business and start building it up again.

It had become clear that she would never reach her goals if she depended on the income the portrait studio was providing. She wanted to continue to focus on providing a quality service while also exploring other options.

Kyle realized that she needed some help at the studio to be able to extract herself from the daily workflow. One of the most time-absorbing tasks she was doing on a daily basis was editing the images in Photoshop. Once a client decided which photos they wanted as prints or digital files, she would clean them up by removing dust spots, adjusting levels, doing color correction, and removing any blemishes.

So over to job-posting site Elance.com Kyle went, where she started studying the different kinds of tasks VAs there might be able to help with. It wasn't long before she was on a full-blown hunt for a VA that could do some of the post-shoot work for her.

She found plenty of people with experience and hired two photo editing VAs. Within a week or so, her own workload had been significantly reduced.

Kyle's Hurdles

Even though the VAs were starting to save Kyle time, she had issues with some of the virtual workers doing too much retouching or color correction, resulting in her photographs looking somewhat strange or unnatural.

She hired another VA and gave him work for a few months on a job-by-job basis—but he kept raising his prices. So Kyle decided to move on and try others.

This is one of the downfalls of working with freelancers regularly: They get to know that you like them and some start taking advantage of that fact.

Kyle believed in the process and kept hiring, in an effort to learn what made for the best relationship and experience working with virtual staff. She tried hiring independents, then freelancers who were part of agencies. She took the time to evaluate different scenarios and compare the results.

One of the things she had to do was to make allowances for things taking longer than she was expecting.

One VA in the Philippines had a job to do for her, re-touching 300 images in three days. The VA, Angie, said she could do it—"No problem, Boss!"—but two days into the project Kyle couldn't get a response via Skype or e-mail. The deal was looming, the client was e-mailing Kyle about the finished work, and Angie was nowhere to be found. In the end, Kyle had to finish the job herself.

Two days later Angie appeared, pinging and dinging Kyle's inboxes everywhere: "We had a power outage, we could not reach out at all, sorry, Boss."

A couple of really important lessons came out of Kyle's initial experiences:

- Three-day deadlines don't really have a place when working with VAs. She decided to always allow more time than she thought the job needed. That meant that there were some tasks that just were not right for sending out, like crazy rush jobs.
- Training someone to do a job like choosing the best 100 images out of 1,000 requires helping them learn how you think. When Kyle hired people on a job-by-job basis, she had to start fresh every time. That's when she decided it would be better to find one good VA and make them very happy to work with her consistently, the same way she operates with her physical staff.

Kyle's Best Practices

To combat the issue of freelancers overworking the photos, Kyle created an in-depth training video using Camtasia, software that allows you to record what's on your computer screen, along with your own audio. This allows her to train the VAs on exactly how she would like things done. It's been a massive help.

Even though she does have a couple of VAs that she works with regularly, nowadays Kyle is now a little more careful when working with freelancers too frequently, preferring to keep her options open, creating an ongoing list of people to work with.

She has worked with eight different VAs over the last couple of years, ranging in experience levels and from countries such as the Philippines, the United Kingdom, and back home in the United States.

In an ongoing effort to continue to create more time in her day, Kyle recently hired a full-time VA to help with the culling of images on an ongoing basis, such as taking 5,000 photos and cutting them down to 100, as well as another virtual assistant to research content ideas for her studio's blog and to help with creating possible leads for corporate photography.

All this means that, along with taking care of her brick-and-mortar photography business, she can now also focus on creating additional streams of income from various online projects—for which she also hires VAs to help her with.

Kyle's Tools of the Trade

Here are the three top tools that Kyle uses when working with her virtual team on a day to day basis:

- **Skype** (Skype.com): Using Skype as a live chat tool seems to be the easiest way for Kyle's VAs to work with her live. They can pass files and images back and forth as they type messages and thoughts.
- **Camtasia** (Techsmith.com/Camtasia): A great way for Kyle's live team to train her virtual team, they create video tutorials showing exactly how to retouch or do a selection process on an image, while describing it at the same time via verbal instructions.
- **Dropbox** (Dropbox.com): Photographs being moved over the Internet take up lots of space. Dropbox is an amazing tool for storing and sharing files around the world—and it's fast, too.

Kyle's story is the perfect example of a brick-and-mortar-business owner using the power of virtual staff in a way that directly creates more time in their business, day to day.

However, what I love about the story more than anything else is that even though she struggled here and there, she saw the value in this concept of working with remote workers. She stuck with it, and it's paid off handsomely.

Best Practices When Training Your Virtual Staff

We've just covered how to set the stage for a big-picture approach to training your virtual staff, so now let's discuss a couple of pretty important best practices that will streamline the process.

Identify Repetitive Tasks

Every position within a company involves activities that need to be done on an ongoing basis. It could be daily, weekly, or even monthly, but these are repetitive tasks that will always need to be done within a particular role.

By taking the time to identify these tasks and to create a simple process for your VA to follow, you'll avoid the frustration that arises if a VA tries to reinvent the wheel or complicate an existing system. Should this happen, you can simply point the VA back to the process map you've already created.

Repetitive tasks might include

- order fulfillment
- purchasing

- blog posting
- research
- social media status updates

Keep in mind that process maps for repetitive tasks should not be complicated. A simple Google Drive document with bullet points or a quick video will work just fine.

Create an IFTTT Cheat Sheet

A good organization that understands its products and services typically has an FAQ section on its website for customers and prospect customers to discover. Don't have one? Put one together!

But what about frequently asked questions that arise within the organization itself? Unless a written set of protocols exists for handling specific situations, employees will create their own ways of doing things.

When VAs encounter situations they don't know how to handle, they're likely to try to figure out their own solutions—adding extra time and potentially resulting in bad decisions. If the VA still can't figure it out or is afraid of making the wrong choice, you'll probably receive an e-mail with one or more questions. If you're in different time zones, it could easily take several rounds of correspondence and an additional twenty-four to forty-eight hours to resolve the problem.

This is where an IFTTT cheat sheet comes in. Simply put, IFTTT means **if that** happens, **then this** needs to happen. This is similar to the previous exercise you completed on identifying repetitive tasks—but in this case, you're identifying repetitive situations.

Consider these examples:

- **A client makes an inquiry about purchasing additional products or services.** Should your VA make suggestions? Should he or she refer the client to someone else?
- **A client sends an e-mail using profanity and is clearly outraged.** Do you want to hear about it, or do you want your VA to follow the standard customer service procedures?
- **A returning client is asking for a discount on his or her next purchase, which happens to be extremely large.** Do you want your VA to address questions about pricing? Should returning clients get special treatment, or should your VA follow the standard pricing model?

Throw Your VA a Curveball

You've probably heard the saying, "Experience is the best teacher." Well, I'd like to make a minor change to that and say that *new experiences* are the best teachers. The muscles in the human body respond to challenge with growth. The same is true of the brain—and the same is true of your VA.

I'm not saying you should be trying to sabotage your staff members with tasks they're not qualified to handle, but occasional challenges are good for them. I call this approach "throwing a curveball."

Here are a few possible results:

- Your VA surprises you and demonstrates that he or she has a hidden talent.

- Your VA learns a new skill that can be used later in your business.
- Your VA is kept on his or her toes.
- You see how your VA responds to a challenge.

Let's say you've hired a VA for the strict role of handling your online customer service tickets and chat support inquiries. The VA has received proper training and knows exactly how to handle each situation that arises. He or she has displayed a strong work ethic and has earned your respect and trust, but now you'd like to expand the VA's expertise and skill set. This is the perfect time to throw a curveball.

Think of something that your VA has never done before that could use his or her existing talents, such as

- Have the VA draw up a survey with questions he or she thinks would be helpful in creating future products. Of course, you should ask the VA to send it through to you for approval before e-mailing it to your clients.
- Ask your VA to put together a list of the most common questions customers are asking, and a list of best answers.
- Request a list of the VA's personal recommendations for your business. This could include potential products, ways to better serve customers, or any tools or training that would help your VA to do his or her job better.

If your organization's goal is to grow, then each of your employees must be growing, too. Always be willing to offer additional training and do what you can to take an active

VIRTUAL FREEDOM

role in your VA's development. This helps your business and will create a sense of loyalty in your VA to your organization.

All of my staff members know that they can never come to me with a problem alone. I don't accept it. When a staff member tells me about a problem, he or she must also present me with at least one possible solution. This is something I communicate clearly, via an operational guidelines document (something every new employee receives). It allows my VAs to own problems as part of their roles and therefore empowers them to figure out solutions on their own.

A VA's solution might not be the perfect way to handle a problem, but I can tell you from experience that more often than not the VA's ideas contribute to the way in which the situation is eventually resolved. Throwing a curveball like this also helps you to stay on the lookout for talented individuals who demonstrate leadership and critical thinking skills. These are the VAs you'll want to consider for future management positions.

Your VA Success Equation

By now, I certainly hope you're beginning to see that using VAs is about more than finding someone to e-mail tasks to. It's about establishing clarity in your business, understanding your needs, and developing a unique way of doing things that you can use to train others.

With that in mind, I've developed what I call the VA Success Equation to harness the power of virtual staff. Before I give it to you, let me show you the typical VA Success Equation to which most virtual newbies subscribe:

→ Entrepreneur + VA = More Productivity, More Time and Money, and Virtual Freedom

Now, this equation does have some truth to it. However, it's missing a few vital components that, if left unaddressed, will leave the entrepreneur frustrated and thinking something is wrong with the VA he or she chose. The missing components are

- clearly defined needs and goals
- training
- focus on high-level priorities

Without taking these things into consideration, the entrepreneur ends up frustrated and thinking, "You see? It's best if I do these things myself."

Here's what the real VA Success Equation looks like:

→ Entrepreneur + Clearly Defined Needs and Goals + VA + Training = More Productivity, More Time to Focus on High-Level Priorities, and More Money and Virtul Freedom

Let's examine each of the components that were missing from the original equation:

- **Clearly Defined Needs and Goals**: Without clearly defined needs and goals, a VA will only be viewed as a cost to your business—and he or she will trigger the micromanaging vulture in you to come out. Refer back to your 3 Lists to Freedom and create a goal to rid yourself of the work that you shouldn't be doing. Remember, your time and attention are needed elsewhere.

- **Training**: By now, you should be starting to understand that training your VA is one of the major keys to success in this whole game. Yes, your VA is already skilled—but it takes time to incorporate him or her into your workflow, and it's impossible to do that without training.

- **Focus on High-Level Priorities**: A lot of people are attracted to the idea of having more time. However, unless they know what they plan to do with that time, it's going to be wasted once it arrives. The best use of extra time is to focus on high-level priorities—but do you know what they are? If you were given an extra two hours today to invest in your business, do you know in which projects or tasks you would invest those hours?

My advice? Treat your extra time like it is another VA. Give it a clearly defined goal and expect progress. Always.

Entrepreneurial podcaster John Lee Dumas has created a monster online library of content with his daily podcast *Entrepreneur On Fire*. John uses several VAs that work with him day-to-day, so that his time is left open to record shows, set up future shows, and generally "be there" for his listeners and mastermind students—his way of turning the content generating machine that he has created into a business for him. He knows the value of his time and makes sure to capitalize on every hour accordingly.

FREEDOM SPOTLIGHT

Pat Flynn

Online Entrepreneur

SmartPassiveIncome.com

You may already be familiar with Pat Flynn's hugely popular website, SmartPassiveIncome.com or his podcast that shares the candid truth about what it takes to create a profitable living online through niche websites, affiliate marketing, and other digital ventures. A dedicated husband and father of two, Pat has struck that coveted work-life balance: spending a great deal of time with his family while also running an extremely successful business. However, it hasn't always been as easy for Pat to operate and build his business empire as it is today.

⟩ The Problem

It took Pat some time before he recognized he was going to need help running his burgeoning business. On a daily basis he was burning the candle at both ends, juggling graphic design (which he's actually pretty good at), some web coding (which he's not so good at!), and everything else that goes along with creating and growing a highly respected brand—superhero syndrome in full effect. What ultimately drove him to seek out a VA was spending two-and-a-half months recording an audio book version of a popular e-book he had penned before learning the hard way that he simply was not a legitimate voice actor or sound designer. Once he figured this out, he scrapped the entire project.

⟩ The Solution

After seeking advice from a friend, Pat used Elance.com to seek out a voice talent who would record the book for him. At that point, Pat took notice of the enticing possibilities of working with virtual staff. It was obvious that he couldn't manage all the different areas of his business on his own, and he didn't even have some of the skill sets required to keep it up and running fully. Pat turned to Virtual Staff Finder to find a seasoned web developer and a general VA to help him take things to the next level—which is exactly what happened.

The Outcome

Although he loved his virtual workers on the other side of the world, Pat has since moved to hiring only domestically. Today, Pat is still taking full advantage of virtual staff, but they're all based—as he is—in the United States. His team includes virtual staff members who work on a part-time or project basis and VAs who handle everything from event coordination to transcription work. He prefers to have his team a little closer to home because he enjoys the face-to-face interaction that he creates at regular, in-person meetings at intervals throughout the year.

SECTION THREE

Managing Your Virtual Staff

Getting your virtual staffing program past the hiring and training phases is similar to the takeoff of an airplane—it takes a lot of energy and attention to detail to get started, but everything is easier to navigate once you reach the proper altitude and start heading in the right direction. Once you're at that optimum altitude, it's time to talk about management.

This is where small adjustments will make a huge impact on your team's productivity. It's also where you'll build a customized system that will keep things moving forward.

In this section, we'll cover

- how to manage the different types of VAs
- revolving tasks and projects
- how to use project-management software
- generating reports with your virtual staff
- best practices for paying and motivating your VAs

Before we dive in, I'd like to discuss one of the most common mistakes I see people make with their virtual assistants.

Don't Be a Virtual Vulture

There's a strange phenomenon that occurs among entrepreneurs when they begin delegating tasks and projects to virtual assistants: the entrepreneurs transform into virtual vultures. Let's take a look at the typical behavior of these micromanaging creatures.

Virtual vultures have been known to use screen capture software to monitor a VA's computer to see if he or she is working. The entrepreneur harbors nagging feelings of unease and thinks, "Why did I hire a VA when I could easily be doing this work myself?" or, "I really hope the VA isn't screwing things up right now." Worst of all, the entrepreneur constantly interrupts the VA to ask if he or she needs any help—even though the VA hasn't asked for it.

When this type of thinking takes hold, it's only a matter of time before superhero syndrome kicks in and you start telling yourself, "I should probably call off this whole virtual assistant thing and get back to business as usual, handling things myself. I can do this work better and faster than anyone else. And even if I don't know how to do something, I can always teach myself and save a ton of money! Besides, who knows if the VA is really doing all the work I've assigned? I'd better keep a close eye out."

And that's how the virtual vulture emerges. It spreads its wings and hovers over every move your team makes. The only thing this accomplishes is nurturing a lack of trust, which will ultimately keep you from leading your team properly.

I've seen a lot of people fail to make the transition from

solopreneur (working entirely on their own and handling every bit of work on a day-to-day basis) to virtual CEO because they've embraced the virtual vulture.

I'm not saying you should just assign tasks and walk away—because that's just as bad. Instead, you need to develop a management process that incorporates

- a clear objective—vagueness is your enemy
- examples of what you want—offering examples is like giving your VA a target
- benchmarks and checkpoints along the way that will help you see if the VA is making progress and staying on track
- the freedom for the VA to do his or her job—or to demonstrate that he or she isn't a good fit. I'll explain this one in detail in just a bit, so keep reading.

As you can see, there's a process to production. Let's take a closer look at each of these elements.

1. A Clear Objective

If you can't articulate what you want, there's no way your VA can be expected to give you what you want. Right? Right!

Now, I know there's going to be times when you really don't know what you want, and that's why you've hired a VA—to create the work and give you ideas. If this is the case, you'll need to understand a couple things:

- Don't expect your VA to get it right the first time. If you give your VA a few ideas and tell him or her to run with them, then understand that your first phase is a discovery process so that the VA can figure out exactly what you want.

- Even if your VA is giving you ideas and concepts, it's still your responsibility to give direction and to narrow down the process to a clear objective.

Here are a few tips on developing and delivering clear task and project objectives to your VA:

- **Use bullet points.** Bullet points force you to break down your ideas and give your VA a checklist to reference. They're also easy on the eyes.
- **Ask yourself how the project or task can be measured.** How many pages do you want your website to have? What colors should your logo contain? How many different options should the VA give you when doing online research? What five points should the article include? How long do you want the video to be?
- **Share the overall objective.** Even if a VA is working on just one piece of a larger puzzle—such as a graphic designer creating custom images for your website—it's helpful to share the overall objective with him or her. Let your VA know what the purpose of the website is and give him or her a description of your ideal client. All of these clues will affect the outcome of your project.

2. Examples of What You Want

Once you have a clear objective in mind, your next step is to give your VA specific examples of what you want.

Giving your VA an example is like giving him or her a target to shoot at. You'll be the judge of whether or not your VA hits the bull's-eye, but at least you'll get him or her shooting in the right direction. Provide examples for everything and anything and use all types of mediums.

This means you should feel free to

- Take a picture of a product's packaging in a store and use it as an example of how you'd like your digital product images to look.
- Send your VA a link to an article you recently read and let him or her know what you liked about it and what aspects you'd like to see incorporated into future articles you request.
- Send your VA a YouTube video as an example of the type of editing you'd like to see.
- Use a flyer as an example of the type of layout you'd like your website to have.
- If you see a piece of clothing or a car with a color you like, take a picture of it so that your VA can incorporate the color into a logo design or image.
- If you hear a song and think it would make great background music for your video, send a sample of it to your VA and ask him or her to find something similar to use in the editing process.

3. Benchmarks and Checkpoints

As I mentioned earlier, the last thing you'll want to do is assign a task or project and then walk away and wait for it to be completed. There are hundreds—if not thousands—of decisions that go into creating something, which means it's very easy to get off track. Benchmarking is the most powerful technique you can use to keep your virtual vulture at bay because it presents a clear picture of how your project is coming along.

Just as mountain climbers set multiple safety hooks as they climb to prevent complete free falls, you can use benchmarks with your virtual staff to prevent large mistakes and failures in your project.

Benchmarking is useful for VAs, and it is also helpful for you as an outsourcer. The process forces you to think of the task or project in smaller pieces that fit together, which can help you to focus your objective.

But wait! What if you don't really understand all of the moving parts that go into completing a project? How can you expect yourself to set proper benchmarks in an area you don't really understand?

Let's say you're working with a programmer to design a custom piece of software, such as a mobile app. You know exactly what you'd like the software to do, but you have no idea what's involved in getting it done.

Here's a two-step trick you can use to figure out guidelines for your benchmarks:

1. **Get as clear as you can about your desired objective or outcome.** What do you want the

software to do? What type of experience should the user have? These nontechnical questions will ultimately direct the development.

2. **Put your project on Elance or oDesk with your objective and ask anyone who bids on it to answer the following questions:**

    *   How long do you think this project will take to complete?
    *   Break down the project into benchmarks or steps. How long will you take to complete each one?

By doing this, you're allowing potential VAs to tell you how long it will take to get this project completed—along with the most important benchmarks they should be hitting. But the real beauty of this strategy is that you'll be able to see the average time and common benchmarks proposed from multiple VAs. This information will educate you and equip you to set proper expectations for you and the VA you choose.

4. The Freedom for the VA to Do His or Her Job

Once you've given your VA a clear objective, examples of what you want, and several benchmarks to hit, your next job is to get out of the way. You hired this person for a reason—to do a job and to be responsible enough to keep himself or herself on task. Now is the time to let your VA loose and see what he or she does with that freedom.

Does your VA hit the benchmarks on time? Does he or

she come back with questions after getting stuck? Or does your VA wait until you follow up on a benchmark only to tell you that the task isn't completed because he or she didn't understand it?

These are the kinds of habits you won't see if you're a virtual vulture. You're hiring someone for his or her time, talents, and ability to actually do the work. It does you no good to have someone on your team who is talented but requires constant supervision to get things done.

With that said, here are some tips to help you manage your VA:

- Tell your VA to come to you with any questions at any time. Let the VA know that if you don't hear from him or her, you will expect that everything is okay and that the next benchmark will be hit as scheduled.
- If your VA misses a benchmark, make sure to ask what prevented him or her from meeting the deadline. Find out if your VA will need more time to hit the next benchmark.
- If your VA does not deliver work on the set benchmark date and did not inform you of the delay, do not contact him or her. Wait for the VA to contact you and immediately address the missed date. Let him or her know that you expect the next benchmark to be different.

These three tips will allow you be a fair manager who doesn't have to micromanage, get angry, or use harsh words to get things done.

If you find yourself becoming repeatedly angry with a virtual employee about his or her work or work ethic, it's time to let that person go. There's no need to use anger to get things done, and there are too many great virtual workers out there to waste your time with someone who keeps dropping the ball.

Now, let's look at some specific tips for managing each role.

CASE STUDY #5

Steve Dixon, Serial Entrepreneur
Dixon Clothing Group and Breakthrough4Business

Currently running two separate businesses, Steve Dixon is quite the entrepreneur. In just ten years, Steve's first company, Dixon Clothing Group—which specializes in creating custom sport and school uniforms—has grown into a seven-figure business with a staff of forty people in four different countries. Steve's second endeavor, Breakthrough4Business (Breakthrough4Business.com.au), helps business owners grow and learn through four annual events featuring remarkable speakers from around the world and through ongoing monthly coaching.

After about five years of determinedly attempting to run two businesses on his own, Steve finally realized he could use a little help. Initially, he didn't consider using virtual staff—but after some wise counsel from a trusted industry speaker, Dale Beaumont, Steve joined Virtual Staff Finder and ended up hiring four virtual assistants from the Philippines.

Why Virtual Staffing?

While many entrepreneurs and business owners choose not to mix work with their personal lives, Steve's two businesses were founded and run on integrity and personal values, so Steve quickly realized that the family-oriented attitudes of his VAs were highly valuable assets to his companies.

His staff members consist of two GVAs, a web developer, and an SEO/Internet marketing VA who focuses on web analytics and reporting. They are all highly qualified, but that doesn't stop Steve from stepping in and giving the odd training session as and when he feels it's needed. Steve's virtual employees are good at what they do and have complementary skill sets, making for a harmonious, efficient work environment. It's clear that his VAs find it rewarding to be part of such a well-oiled team because they are eager to prove how capable they are. This allows Steve to focus on the developmental aspect of his business while his staff takes care of the technical side.

VAs that work on the Dixon Clothing Group side of Steve's empire maintain relationships with suppliers and interact with them to ensure that orders are completed correctly. They also update and maintain all of his related websites and help on social media promotions.

For his training and coaching business, the VAs predominantly update and maintain the Breakthrough-4Business website and ensure that the database is constantly upgraded and up to date.

Steve's Hurdles

Steve recognized early on that he himself was the biggest obstacle to overcome as he ventured into outsourcing. He needed to learn how to fully embrace and trust his VAs as an extension of himself rather than seeing them as hired help. Rather than leaving this important decision up to chance, Steve appreciated Virtual Staff Finder's ability to let him take control of the situation through Skype interviews and handpicked assistants.

Steve's Best Practices

- **Value your VAs.** Steve can't emphasize enough the importance of treating each VA as a valid, integral part of the team. When so much of your business is entrusted to your VAs, you can't afford to mistreat or underestimate them. Though they may be half-way around the world, you should still value them as you would value your colleagues in surrounding cubicles.
- **Give meaningful tasks.** Because your staff is out of sight, it may be difficult to avoid the "out of mind" attitude. Steve maintains that you should keep your VAs busy with meaningful tasks in order to keep the full weight of the burden off your shoulders and to keep your staff productive and purposeful. It's a win-win!

Steve's Tools of the Trade

Here are the top tools Steve employs when working with his virtual staff:

- **Teamwork Project Manager** (TeamworkPM.net): Software that is perfect for allocating tasks, managing projects, and keeping your staff on the same page.
- **Jing** (Techsmith.com/Jing): A fantastic program that allows for simultaneous screen captures and audio and video recording, making your instructions and goals simple and clear.

How to Manage Different VA Roles

What we just covered were the basic principles of VA management that can be applied to any role within your business. Now we'll get down to the nitty-gritty, beginning with a look at the many different types of VA roles you can add to your arsenal.

You'll see that there are specific tips to manage productivity within each role without turning you into a sleepless worrywart.

General Virtual Assistant (GVA)

- Create a shared Google Drive document to track hours and activities.
- Get on a consistent schedule of checking in with your GVA. I recommend twice per week.
- When you e-mail a new task to your GVA, write "NEW TASK: (Enter Task Title)" in the subject line. Then have your VA enter this task into the shared document for tracking.
- Pay biweekly. Your GVA will appreciate it and will be eager to keep working with you.

Tools and Resources

The following are a few resources that help GVAs manage their day-to-day activities and make them better at what they do for you. Simply suggesting these (and any other that you may find on your own) is all you need to do—most of the time—to get your GVA to buy into wanting to better himself or herself. A short e-mail is all that it takes, such as:

Hi Melanie

I found these resources online while searching for ways for us to become super-productive together as a team. Thought I'd share them with you.

- *Resource #1*
- *Resource #2*
- *Resource #3*

I particularly like [Resource #2], as it showed how you can [activity] to help the business become more productive/profitable.

Check them out and let me know what you think!

Chris

Here are some excellent resources for GVAs:

- **Home workspace guides**: Check out a great guide from *Inc.* magazine on setting up a professional, productive workspace at home at Inc.com/Guides/Set-Up-A-Home-Office.html and find another great collection of articles on setting up a home office from *Entrepreneur* magazine at Entrepreneur.com/HomeOffice/.
- **Virtual assistant training course**: Over fifteen hours of training and more than seventy-five videos aimed at Filipino GVAs (VirtualStaff TrainingAcademy.com).
- **Training for administrative assistants**: A training hub full of valuable resources from the Association of Administrative Assistants (AAA.ca).
- **Training and more free tools**: Mind Tools (MindTools.com) has a collection of some brilliant training courses and free tools.

The following tools are also absolute necessities when it comes to the day-to-day management of GVAs—and almost every other type of virtual worker, too!

- **Google Drive** (Google.com/Drive): Shared Excel and Word documents are a great place to upload new tasks and manage weekly hours.

- **Dropbox** (Dropbox.com): A must-have productivity tool. This is where you'll want your VA sending research and uploading and sharing media files.

- **Skype** (Skype.com): A lot of virtual CEOs recommend using Skype to stay connected with virtual staff members. Depending on the times of day you and your GVA work, there may be an overlap where you can find time to chat or go through any questions. For face-to-face interaction with more than just one staff member, I suggest Google Hangouts.

Web Developer

- Search online and give your developer examples of what you have in mind for your website.

- Always keep the user experience in mind. Your job is to communicate a clear user experience to your developer, and the developer's job is to make that happen.

- Get on Skype or the phone to discuss your project. Some things are better communicated with a quick conversation than through e-mail.

- Ask your developer for suggestions on plugins and other tech-y subjects.

Tools and Resources

As most web developers are already very experienced, I've decided to list some resources for *you* here, intended as a primer to the worlds of web design and programming. I've included a few extra tips for hiring, too. These resources won't make you a pro overnight, but they will help you understand the basics and learn to speak the developer's language.

- **List of web-design terms**: The easy-to-understand list from Hubspot (http://blog.hubspot.com/non-designers-web-design-glossary) will make sense of most of the words you'll hear tossed around in the web development world.
- **Hiring guide**: *Inc.* magazine's guide to hiring a web developer is available at Inc.com/Guides/Web-Developer-Hire.html.
- **Project-management tool**: Basecamp (Basecamp.com) is a great piece of software that is perfect for project-based work when you need to keep everyone on the same page. There are also a few different options that I'll go into in a little more detail soon. However, if you're using a platform like Elance to work with project-based freelancers, they'll already have a management tool like this built into their own systems.

Graphic Designer

- Even if you lack a creative eye, you can still direct your graphic designer by giving him or her examples of what you're looking for.

- Have your GVA search through online image libraries such as iStock (iStockphoto.com).
- Be as specific as possible when giving details; when providing color preferences, for example, use exact HTML color codes.
- Fonts are a major aspect of design work, and it'll help your designer substantially if you have an idea of the type(s) of font(s) you would like featured. I like to take snapshots with my phone of any cool fonts I see when I'm out and about. Even if my graphic designer can't match it perfectly, he'll get pretty close!

Tools and Resources

In addition, here are a few tools and resources you can pass on to your graphic designer to help him or her find ideas:

- **IconArchive** (IconArchive.com): Huge collection of web icons.
- **Web design ideas**: Two fantastic galleries of brilliant website designs are available at TheBest Designs.com and Great-Web-Design.net.
- **Design Cubicle** (TheDesignCubicle.com): Design news, opinions, and portfolio links.
- **99designs** (99designs.com): Lots of graphic artists come here to showcase their work.

SEO/Internet Marketing VA

- Spend time figuring out very clearly what keywords you want to target. What phrases will your potential customers search for? Because you understand the needs of your market best, you'll need to figure out the initial answers to this question.

- Ask your SEO VA for a strategy and what results he or she hopes to get.

- Keep an eye on your site's analytics. Though you should be reasonable with the timeframe before expecting to see results, working with an SEO VA should result in a rise in traffic. Check up on your progress every two weeks.

- Ask your SEO VA how he or she stays current and up to date with Google algorithm changes.

- Keep an eye on your site's highest-ranking words and phrases. Ask yourself, "Are these the phrases my customers would search for?" It doesn't help you one bit to have a top ranking for a phrase or word that no one is trying to find. Don't be fooled by these kinds of results.

- Keep an open line of communication with your VA—and if you don't see results, find someone new. Yes, it takes time to see changes, but there should be results after awhile.

Tools and Resources

- **SEO glossary** (SEOBook.com/Glossary): A thorough list of terms to give you a basic working knowledge of SEO. Even I'm still learning!

- **Quick-start SEO (for you, not your VA)**: A must-read article from *Entrepreneur* magazine on the subject of protecting yourself from SEO companies that promise the world and more is available at Entrepreneur.com/Article/204594.

- **Market Samurai** (MarketSamurai.com): A great keyword research and optimization tool.
- **Long Tail Pro** (LongTailPro.com): Another fantastic keyword research tool that recently has been used more and more by big-name bloggers and Internet marketers.

Content Writer

- Work with multiple writers. Each writer has his or her own style, and it takes a little time to find the ones you like. It's also a good idea to work with multiple writers in the event that one of them falls through and you need to send work to someone else.
- Provide your writers with the main points you'd like them to cover in the articles they're writing for you.
- Give a word count—typical blog posts are 500 to 1,000 words in length.
- If you want to write articles yourself, hire a copy editor. A copy editor will proofread your work and can even tighten up loosely written pieces. Writing a loose piece is a great way for you to create content without spending a lot of time on multiple drafts. You simply write a rough draft as quickly as you can and then hand it over to a copy editor or one of your writers to improve.

MANAGING YOUR VIRTUAL STAFF

Tools and Resources

- **Evernote** (Evernote.com): This program allows users to take notes though text, audio, photos, and video and then sync the information across all their digital devices. Users can then search their notes using keywords, just as they would search on the Internet. This means there's no reason for any idea for a new piece of content to slip through the cracks.

- **Plagiarism Checker** (PlagiarismChecker.com): The Internet makes it very easy to copy work from other people. As you work with your writer, I urge you at least periodically check his or her work to make sure it is original. Doing so can be a lifesaver, especially when working with freelancers that you don't know well.

- **Simplenote** (Simplenote.com): This is one of my favorite mobile apps. I have it installed on my iPhone and my iPad, and I use to it make notes about potential new content ideas. Sometimes I use it to type out entire blog posts while I'm waiting in line or sitting in an airport lounge and I don't want to have to dive into my bag for my laptop. You can also give your writer direct access to the work you've produced so that he or she can tweak and elaborate on it.

Video Editor

It will be helpful for you, your editor, and your brand if your videos follow a consistent pattern. This will allow your editor to get into a rhythm since he or she will know exactly what you're looking for.

I also recommend giving your editor the following items:

- Your script—or at least a brief bullet point list of how you'd like everything put together.
- What kind of music you want (if any).
- Which take of each scene to include in the final clip.

Tools and Resources

- **Storyboard template**: A quick search on Google Images will bring up a lot of different options. My advice is to keep your storyboard simple and effective. You print it, doodle away, and make any additional notes for your VA to take into consideration when editing. Then snap a photo on your phone, upload it to Dropbox for the VA, and get to work.
- **Web2Explosion** (Web2Explosion.com): Amazing collection of Web 2.0 icons and buttons that your editor can use in your online videos.
- **Splasheo** (Splasheo.com): This service is run by Gideon Shalwick, one of the biggest names in online video. His company produces insanely high-quality video bumpers to use at the beginnings and ends of your videos in addition to many other products. I personally use these guys.

App Developer

- Try to have an understanding of which device(s) you'll actually want your app to be launched on before hiring an app developer. Consider the demographic you're targeting, how people will actually use the app, and other factors to determine what type of app you need.

- Hire an app developer with whom you can easily communicate. This may mean keeping things closer to home or finding an overseas developer who speaks English well and always get back to you in a timely fashion.

- The best, most successful apps are those that do one thing really, really well. Point this out to your developer and have him or her really focus in on your core usability factor. It'll solve a lot of issues that might occur later on.

Tool and Resources

- **ShoutEm** (Shoutem.com): Mashable.com said that this great little service is "as simple as it can be." This is the way to go if you're still fighting superhero syndrome and trying to create mobile apps yourself. You can also simply hand it off to your app developer to peruse.

- **MobileDevHQ** (MobileDevHQ.com): A lot of great developers are excellent on the building side of things but lack marketing knowledge. These guys help out with publicizing and advertising your app.

- **IconBeast** (IconBeast.com): Amazing collection of mobile icons that can be used across all major mobile devices. Regardless of the category, there's something here for every app.

The Difference Between Revolving Tasks and Projects

Now that you have specific tips, tools, and resources to manage each of the primary outsourced roles, let's discuss the two different types of work you'll be managing: revolving tasks and projects.

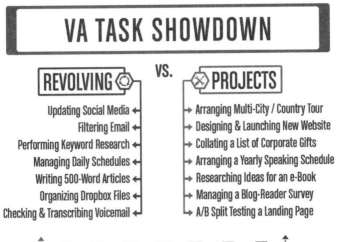

VA TASK SHOWDOWN

REVOLVING vs. **PROJECTS**

REVOLVING	PROJECTS
Updating Social Media	Arranging Multi-City / Country Tour
Filtering Email	Designing & Launching New Website
Performing Keyword Research	Collating a List of Corporate Gifts
Managing Daily Schedules	Arranging a Yearly Speaking Schedule
Writing 500-Word Articles	Researching Ideas for an e-Book
Organizing Dropbox Files	Managing a Blog-Reader Survey
Checking & Transcribing Voicemail	A/B Split Testing a Landing Page

Revolving Tasks

Revolving tasks are activities performed on a consistent basis that must follow a set schedule, often occurring daily, weekly, monthly, or quarterly.

A few examples include

- sending out daily tweets and updating Facebook pages
- performing keyword research for articles
- writing 500-word blog posts for niche content
- filtering your e-mail before getting started every day
- compiling a list of daily meetings each morning
- sending "Happy Birthday" e-mails to your clients

First, you'll need to identify the revolving tasks in your business. Let me give you a piece of advice: before you start assigning daily, weekly, and monthly tasks, you need to get brutally honest about the goals of your business and why each of these tasks is necessary to move things forward. Creating work for the sake of feeling productive is the last thing you want to do.

Once you've identified your revolving tasks, your next step is to create a revolving task calendar to outline the schedule you want your VAs to follow. This calendar should illustrate exactly what you want and when you want it done. If you'd like to take it one step further, I recommend including quarterly tasks as well. However, even if you don't have any quarterly revolving tasks, this exercise will help you to start thinking strategically.

Here's an example of a revolving task template I use for my social media activity on a weekly basis with one of my general VAs.

Day of the Week	Type of Update	Platform/ Channel
Monday	video clip	Facebook, Twitter, Google+
Tuesday	question	Facebook, Twitter, LinkedIn
Wednesday	article/resource	Facebook, Twitter, Google+
Thursday	success quote	Twitter, Google+
Friday	podcast promo	Facebook, Twitter, Google+, LinkedIn
Saturday	personal update	Facebook, Twitter
Sunday	business quote	Facebook, Twitter, Google+, LinkedIn

You can clearly see that my social media focus is on Facebook and Twitter. Although it's wise to have profiles set up everywhere, I've found it's better to focus on just a couple.

The different types of updates I have my VA put together allow me to look professional, but also varied in my approach when connecting with readers, clients, and subscribers.

You can download this revolving task template by visiting the book website, **VirtualFreedomBook.com/Reader**

Projects

Projects are activities that have clear beginnings and ends, such as building a website, creating and sending your clients a survey, or booking a flight.

The first step to successful project management is to prioritize. This is why I recommend that you ask yourself the following questions:

1. **Which projects will have the greatest impact on my business?** Try to identify at least two potential outcomes of each project.

2. **How much time and money will it take to complete these projects?** If you don't know, figure it out!

You can now start mapping out your project calendar. This is where Google Drive documents can be used to track projects and set benchmarks. Additionally, you can use project-management software like Asana, HiveDesk, or the aforementioned Basecamp. As project-management software is usually a little foreign to first-timers, allow me to briefly explain what it's all about and what it can bring to the table in regard to the day-to-day management of your virtual staff.

It's amazing how many decisions and moving parts are needed to complete even the smallest projects. Take, for example, ordering a sandwich.

Let's say you sent your personal assistant to the nearest sandwich shop to pick up a quick lunch for you. The next thing out of your PA's mouth would probably be the following barrage of questions—especially if he or she wanted to please you: "Meat or vegetarian? If meat, what kind of meat(s)? Bread choice? Toasted bread? Cheese? Lettuce, spinach, or both? Tomatoes? Salt and pepper or just one of them? Mustard, mayonnaise, ketchup, or dry? Onions? Cut the sandwich diagonally, straight across, or leave it whole?"

It takes a lot of small decisions to complete even the easiest of projects. In the sandwich metaphor, you're working with just one personal assistant who's going to work with one sandwich maker. A project you undertake for your business is likely to be much more complicated, with multiple layers that require multiple people to put that "sandwich" together.

This is where project-management software can help. It makes keeping all those people and pieces of a project organized, on task, and on schedule. Before VAs arrived in your life, you probably didn't need it: you were the main sandwich maker in your business—and you were probably your own personal assistant, too. Sure, things were hectic and crazy, but you were always making progress (even if it was slow) and you knew exactly where you were in any given project.

But now that your virtual workers are on the scene, things are different. You've traded your role as a sandwich maker to become a project manager—and that can get complicated if you don't have a system in place to juggle everything. So let's go into the different project-management software options available to you and your virtual team.

Using Project-Management Software

Allow me to begin with a disclaimer: you don't *need* project-management software if you don't want it. However, you do need a project-management system.

Multiple VAs + Multiple Projects = High Probability of Missing Something

There's no way you can prevent details from falling through the cracks or expect to get multiple projects completed on time without a system in place.

As I mentioned earlier, your project-management system could be as simple as a shared Google Drive document, which is actually quite effective—or it could be a bit more complex like any one of the project-management software solutions I'm about to introduce. It just needs to be a place where you can assign responsibilities to every member of your team and where they can share how their work is coming along. The benefit to the software, though, is that you can stay on the same page with your team by checking in on the software instead of following up with each person individually.

Another advantage to project-management software is that it allows you to communicate within the software itself. This is awesome, as it cuts down on e-mail—always welcome! Instead of e-mailing files or using Dropbox, you can upload files directly via the software, and they are time-stamped, so you can see when your project was last updated.

Here are a few project-management software solutions that I recommend and the main features of each.

Basecamp—Basecamp.com

- View everything on a single page, including a snapshot overview of all your projects.
- Receive a daily update of all activity performed on all projects.

- Share files within the platform and minimize your need for Dropbox.
- Organize your team into different groups or projects.
- See each person's calendar and what he or she is working on.

Asana—Asana.com

- Enjoy free access!
- Assign, follow, and comment on tasks.
- Set milestones, priorities, and due dates.
- Create custom views of your team's work and search through and filter results.
- Receive notifications on your smartphone or mobile device of updated projects and completed work.

Teamwork Project Management—TeamworkPM.net

- Create and assign task lists to individual team members.
- Create and track milestones.
- Reveal tasks and projects to the appropriate team members through special privacy settings. This feature is especially helpful if you're working on several projects with a number of different virtual workers.
- Shared notebook writing allows multiple members to contribute to one piece of content in one place, working like an in-house Google Drive document.
- Categorize messages for easy searching.

HiveDesk—HiveDesk.com

- Check in and out throughout the day.
- Switch between projects and let the software track the time each worker spends.
- Allocate a single task to a virtual worker or a larger project to a team of people.
- Export work history in PDFs for convenient reporting.
- See random shots of your VA's screen through screen capture technology.

Even though each of these platforms offers slightly different features, the objective of each one is the same—to help virtual teams stay on the same page. Keep in mind that the software just captures everything that's going on—it doesn't directly make people more productive! The real magic happens when you secure the right people for your team, select the right projects, and then work together to lead and complete those projects.

Reports from Your Virtual Staff

Regardless of the size of your virtual team, productivity will be measured by how well team members use regular reports to keep you up to date with everything that's going on. Keeping your team on task and moving in the right direction will result in enormous benefits for your business. However, as I mentioned earlier, you won't accomplish these benefits by becoming a virtual vulture—you'll achieve them through systems and protocol. Success is achieved by fighting superhero syndrome!

Now that you've identified the different types of VAs you can work with, listed your revolving tasks, and prioritized your major projects in a shared calendar (whether it be inside a project-management system or an online calendar like Google Calendar), it's time to create your reporting process.

Don't Worry—It's Not More Work

The first reaction I typically get when I bring up the topic of reporting is, "Wait a second here, Chris—reporting? I don't want to create more work for myself." Don't worry. This isn't going to create more work for you; it's going to help. Effective reporting is the vehicle that will allow you to

- motivate your virtual staff to make daily measurable progress
- answer any questions that arise or bring up any problems
- invite suggestions from your team of ways to do things better

Without a reporting process in place, it's going to be hard to tell if your team is moving in the right direction, prompting your virtual vulture to swoop in for the kill. So here's what you're going to do: For the first thirty days of a new VA's employment, have him or her send you a report at the end of each workday that answers the following questions:

- **What did you accomplish today?** Just imagine if you had a large consulting client asking you this question. I'm not saying you'd like it, but I'm sure it would create a sense of accountability if you had to answer this question each day.

- **Is there anything you need help with or do you have questions?** This gives your VA a safe environment in which to ask for help. As I mentioned earlier, your VA wants to please you and would rather figure things out on his or her own than ask for help.

- **Do you have any suggestions?** Asking your virtual staff for suggestions allows you to see your business through fresh eyes. Your VA is in the trenches of your business each day and can offer valuable insight. Your superhero syndrome would lead you to believe that no one knows your business better than you, but this is not the case in areas that fall outside your expertise.

These are the three topics I have each of my VAs address in an e-mail each day so that I can answer questions and monitor progress. Here's an e-mail report that came in from one of my VAs a few days ago. I haven't changed anything—even the typos!

Hi Boss!

I hope you've had a pleasant day.

Have you checked the Google Analytics report from yesterday? If there are more details you'd like to have added, please let me know. For the next report, I am thinking of adding a backlinks count, but I still have to do an SEO Audit before I can do that.

Meanwhile, I've uploaed the Content Calendar for June, for Chris-Ducker.com to Dropbox. The content syndication and repurposing plan is on the Google Doc we were looking at earlier in the week.

Today I took care of the following:

- *Searched for a infographic designer. Will submit options by end of the week.*
- *Put together the first draft for the new site launch PR.*
- *Facebook tweetable images uploaded (2).*
- *Added more keywords to the blog content list.*
- *Finished the YouTube keyword research. It's in Dropbox.*

Please note on YouTube, I did research for ways to do effective keyword research for YouTube and found many sites that recommend it's Suggest feature. That's why I don't have global and local figures. I also used the advanced features of some popular videos to find keywords.

Please take a look and let me know what you think.

Thanks!
Marie :-)

Marie always signs her e-mails with a smiling emoticon! It's part of her personality, which I like to promote. Now sit back and look at that e-mail again. While I was working on my business, Marie was busy working in it. She took care of all those tasks for me while I focused on clients, internal management meetings, and planning a company event.

After all these years of working with VAs, it's e-mails like this that still blow me away. I get pumped at the thought that my VAs are being so productive, while I—as the business owner and the driving force behind my company's continued growth and success—take care of business.

Once you've established this routine for thirty days, your VA will understand your value progress. You can then decide to move these e-mails to a weekly or bi-weekly schedule.

Justin Fulcher
Online Service Provider
Kinda IT

It's impressive enough that Justin Fulcher is, at this writing, twenty-one years old and running a highly successful business. And when you realize he's been doing it for seven years, you'll wonder why you weren't as proactive when you were a teenager! With essentially no business experience, Justin took to the Internet and found Elance.com, a website for helping freelancers find work, and got to work himself—teaming up with people from all around the world.

› The Problem

After four years of juggling classes and his business, Justin decided to drop out of school and pursue his true passion—world travel. However, in order to recognize this dream, he knew he needed to be 100 percent hands-off in his business so that he could trust his employees to efficiently run the company. Justin's biggest hurdles as he hired virtual staff stemmed from his age and lack of experience. He initially believed the most sensible route was to hire people for the lowest prices possible. However, he quickly learned that the lowest prices tended to result in the lowest quality, which led to a massive amount of micromanaging.

› The Solution

Because he didn't have the time or resources to open a physical office, Justin looked into hiring virtual assistants so that he could leverage his time between traveling and work. As a programmer, Justin took tools for communication and organization into his own hands and had software developed to support several group video chats at a time—a necessary feature for a business owner with a ballooning staff. He also stopped paying as little as he could and genuinely started paying his staff what they were worth, which has resulted in far better quality people being added to his team.

› The Outcome

Today, Justin has more than sixty virtual staff members—ranging from ad-campaign managers to project managers to graphic designers and living in countries as diverse as Pakistan, Sweden, and Canada. He checks in with his top managers for about two to three hours each month to get a progress report. In these meetings, Justin and his team discuss projected growth, milestone maintenance, and future goals and visions. Justin also uses the meetings to make sure his staff is happy and satisfied. Without his virtual staff, there's no way Justin could juggle his jet-setting lifestyle and his business.

Paying and Motivating Your Virtual Staff

Once you've got your VA(s) up and running, the final element of the plan to manage your virtual staff is to keep people motivated.

Don't worry, my simple four-step approach won't require any more time or money—but it will ensure that your virtual staff maintains a healthy pace of production.

1. Pay What They're Worth

Don't expect to pay $250 a month and then overload an overseas VA with more work than a typical nine-to-five employee would be able to handle within that working period.

The rule of thumb for fair pay in this situation is to spend a bit of time researching what workers in the country you're looking at hiring from expect to get paid, and then act accordingly. However, keep in mind that some skills—as well as the people who possess them—are more valuable than others. With this in mind, your salary ranges will obviously fluctuate based on personal needs, business needs, and sometimes your gut instinct.

2. Pay on Time

Paying on time is a huge motivator. Your VA is working hard to meet the expectations you've set, so make sure you follow through with your salary and payment arrangements. Keep in mind that a lot of home-based workers in the Philippines, for example, have family commitments, such as putting siblings through college or taking care of extended family. The majority of a worker's salary might be spent before it even arrives. Paying your VA on time is a simple motivator—and believe me, you have no idea how much of an impact it makes on him or her as your employee.

3. Treat VAs with Respect

Treat your VA as if he or she is in the office, sitting and working right next to you. Just because your VAs are working more than an arm's length away doesn't make them your slaves—they're your virtual assistants, and they are just as important as any other member of your team.

Simple common sense and respect are all that's needed

to keep your team motivated. Of course, it also pays to consider other ways to incentivize your staff.

4. Evaluate Them Regularly

I evaluate my full-time employees every twelve months. This is not just a formality. It's about spending time to focus entirely on performance, their attitude toward work as a whole, and how their position within the company has evolved over the course of the last year.

It's also at this point that I discuss any salary increases (if relevant), along with plans for the future with the employee, as a member of my team. In my experience, VAs greatly appreciate having the focus on them and what this evaluation stands for, such as an opportunity for a pay increase or promotion. So be sure to perform evaluations regularly.

Paid Holidays

Even if you pay your VA a flat rate every month, that doesn't mean you shouldn't give him or her any holidays or paid vacation time. Be fair. Familiarize yourself with the holidays in the country where your VA lives, and decide which of them you will include in their pay. Be sure to communicate with your VA clearly on this, so as to not upset them with regard to cultural or religious holidays.

You may want to abide by local customs with regard to compensation to gain your workers' loyalty or just promote a sense of well-being in your team. For example, the Philippines has a compulsory "thirteenth month" benefit mandated by the Philippine government. This yearly bonus is paid in the middle of December to all Philippine employees and is prorated back throughout the year. Because your company isn't based in the Philippines, you are not required to pay it to your Filipino employee. I do pay it, however. My VAs are super-appreciative of this fact, and I enjoy putting a smile on their faces just before the biggest holiday of the year.

Whatever you decide in terms of pay, just be up front about everything, even as early as the interview or hiring stage.

*For an up-to-date listing of all the major public holidays in many different countries around the world, check out **TimeAndDate.com/Holidays**.*

Health Insurance

If the members of your virtual team are employed full-time, chances are good that they are not working for anyone else and therefore don't have an employer providing them with health insurance. It's a shame, but health insurance is not something that many self-employed virtual employees think about.

I wouldn't suggest that you immediately look into providing health insurance to your virtual workers. However, once you've built up some trust and rapport after a year or so of dedicated full-time employment, you might consider offering health insurance as a bonus or additional perk. It's especially nice for your VAs to have private health insurance in developing countries, such as the Philippines and India for example, because they can include their dependents, such as children and parents, at a low additional cost. If you want to do this for your VA, and they are based in in a different country from the one you live in, ask them to research options and send them through to you, so you can make an informed decision on the topic.

Paying Your Staff and Dealing with Taxes

Almost all of the VAs I've come into contact with prefer to be paid via PayPal. It's instant and it simply works. With PayPal you know where you are, it's trustworthy, and it's a "big" name.

Most freelancers and virtual assistants, no matter where they are based, will be self-employed. Because of this, they will take care of taxes, insurance, pension, etc., themselves.

However, if you ever have any questions in relation to paying taxes and benefits of staff that are overseas, I suggest speaking with an accountant or attorney from your local area, as these things are sometimes worlds apart from one another—especially if your staff is, literally, on the other side of the world.

Because salaries fluctuate quite a bit and the virtual staffing market continues to reshape itself regularly, I've put together a free, online guide for you that I keep up to date at ChrisDucker.com/VAPay.

Get Creative with Bonuses

When it comes to incentives, monetary bonuses are understandably the first thing that comes to mind. I know that a lot of entrepreneurs offer their VAs bonuses via PayPal or other means (Western Union, for example) for a number of reasons, including getting a product launched on time or finalizing a design project. These are all good ideas. Personally I don't like to overdo cash bonuses; if you do it too often and your VA doesn't get one at the end of a particular project, he or she might be a little upset.

Try to get as creative as possible with bonuses and employee gifts. In the past, I've arranged things such as

- iTunes vouchers
- flowers and chocolates on birthdays (ask 'em; they'll tell you when theirs is!)
- overnight stays on wedding anniversaries (they can suggest local hotels)
- baby clothes for a newborn
- restaurant gift certificates (they can send you links of places to check out)
- books arriving out of the blue from Amazon or a similar service

The idea is to motivate and reward your virtual employees so that they work harder, become more productive, and ultimately bring you the ROI that any employer wants—and needs—to see in his or her employees.

Clearly, you can see that there are several aspects to managing your virtual employees effectively. It's not as much of a one-size-fits-all process as a lot of people who talk about it on the Internet might lead you to believe.

Understanding how to manage different types of virtual workers and how to set up a robust reporting process is just the start—but it's a start you need to respect. The bottom line is that if you implement the tried and tested processes I've outlined here, you'll have a much better chance of catapulting your way to virtual freedom than if you just try to wing it.

Your VAs will help you along the way if they are worth their weight. Obviously, you'll want to try to make things gel as early on as possible, regardless of where your VAs are located in the world—which we'll dive into now.

SECTION FOUR

The Big Question: Stay Local or Go Overseas?

One of the biggest questions in the world of virtual staffing is whether you should recruit locally or overseas.

A while back, I was speaking at a conference in the United States in front of around 400 small business owners. At the end of my presentation, we had time for some questions. One gentleman took the microphone and asked how I felt about promoting the idea of taking jobs away from his country.

I pointed out that rather than taking anything away from anyone, a small business can survive its startup phase and eventually create more opportunities for local expansion by enlisting the talents of overseas employees in the beginning.

Though I'm sure the attendee wasn't looking for a fight—nor did I take his line of questioning that way—he did bring up a point that often concerns a lot of people. Both local and offshore talent can effectively deliver the services you need to run, support, and grow your business, no matter where in the world it's based. But there are pros and cons to both types of workers, and that's what we'll be discussing in this section.

This section will cover

- why going overseas may *not* be right for your business
- handling customer support
- the Philippines: an outsourcing dream destination
- five things to remember when working with Filipino VAs

The practice of outsourcing overseas is nothing new. But don't confuse building a team of virtual workers with operating an overcrowded call center or some dingy overseas sweatshop.

The global workforce is expanding faster than we can keep up with it—and sometimes it makes sense to hire overseas workers because of their skill sets and experience rather than their lower hourly rates. That said, sometimes it's prudent to keep things a little closer to home when the time is right or when the task calls for it.

The Advantages of Staying Closer to Home

Remember when you went to college or moved into your own place for the first time and left behind the family home where you grew up? I don't know about you, but I used to go back to that family home each week—sometimes more—for my mother's home-cooked meals.

I also used to go back to talk to my father about business and life. He wasn't a rich man and he didn't have a lot of worldly experience, but he was hardworking and loyal to his employers—and he instilled those qualities in me as a young professional.

Why is it that we prefer to stay close to home when we first go out on our own? In many cases, it's for a sense of comfort and knowing we can depend on those who are closest to us. There's something reassuring in staying close to people who know us, understand our personalities, relate to the ways we communicate, and share a common worldview.

Here's the thing: a lot of people think that in order to take full advantage of outsourcing, they need to have a small army of VAs in a foreign land—but this isn't the case. Sometimes your business is better served by finding local talent instead of venturing overseas.

Here are a few examples of the benefits of working with a local VA:

- **You work in the same time zone.** It may be advantageous to have the same work schedule as your VA so that you can answer questions and/or so that he or she can serve your clients in real time.
- **You need a skilled writer.** Think of your target market or audience for a moment. Would you rather have a foreigner addressing your customers in writing or someone local who understands your cultural mindset and business needs and is also a native speaker of the language? If you're

looking for a copywriter or content writer, I recommend finding someone local. When you need someone to capture your "voice," it makes no sense to venture overseas.

- **You might already like the VA's work.** When you like someone's work, price and location are no longer relevant. Even though I run a VA company and have access to hundreds of employees, I myself will often outsource outside of my own roster of VAs (usually for project-based work) when I like someone's style, background, or simply the way he or she works.

- **The local VA just gets it.** Many business owners I've spoken with say that they prefer to work with domestic VAs simply because they are local. The VAs have the same traditions as their employers and have a better understanding of customers in the country in which the company is based.

Both eaHELP (eaHELP.com) and Zirtual (Zirtual.com) are good solutions for people who want to keep things close to home (in the United States). All of the VAs from these firms are based in the United States, and the companies provide hourly packages to get started—for those flirting with outsourcing for the first time.

Here's a perfect example of when it's best to stay close to home: One of our Virtual Staff Finder clients, a cosmetic surgeon, was working with an SEO VA to optimize his website. The VA had helped the client to rank very well in search engine results—and after some time, our client started getting requests for guest posts from other sites within his niche.

He was interested in writing guest posts because they would increase brand awareness for his clinic—it was essentially free, highly targeted advertising—but he was receiving so many requests that he couldn't keep up. He approached us and asked for a ghostwriter. The client's plan was to focus on finding sites for which he could write guest posts and then have a Filipino VA write the articles. By passing off the writing to a VA, he figured he could take on a large number of guest posts without burning out.

In essence, this isn't a bad strategy. However, hiring an overseas VA wasn't the answer for this client; he needed to write these articles himself or find someone locally to ghostwrite for him. Since the articles would be targeted to an affluent demographic, they needed to be written by someone who could truly understand the mentality of the market. And because they were intended to persuade readers to choose the client's service, the articles needed to sound as though they had been written by someone with experience in the field.

It's important to understand how an overseas VA's culture and experience will affect the work he or she produces. It's not that an overseas VA is incapable or uneducated or won't work hard, but most virtual workers don't think like entrepreneurs—they think like employees. That means you cannot expect them to communicate with the same levels of salesmanship and persuasion that you might be used to.

Why Outsourcing Overseas Is Not for Everyone—or Every Business

During a recent speaking engagement in Australia, a local business owner who was in the middle of seeking bids for a website project approached me. He wanted to monetize the expertise he had acquired while running his cigar shop, so he decided to create an info-product site that would sell a variety of e-books and audio courses about the cigar business. It was clearly a niche topic that required specialized training and knowledge, so I told him it sounded like a good idea and asked how I could help.

He was frustrated because his website was not converting visitors into customers as frequently as he would like. Thanks to outsourcing his media buying, he had great traffic, but the cost per acquisition—or the cost of converting a visitor to a customer—was too high and he simply was not producing a profit.

An outsourcing company based in India had done everything for him, including programming, graphic design, product creation, SEO, copywriting, and pay-per-click management. Since the outsourcing company was 60 percent cheaper than all of the domestic bids he had received, it was initially a clear choice to go overseas. However, the savings didn't matter anymore. His results were terrible, and he wanted my recommendation on finding a new outsourcing company or building a team of VAs himself.

I told him that his problem wouldn't necessarily be solved by finding a new service provider. The problem was that he was making pricing the priority instead of focusing on the necessary roles and skills that would make his website successful.

Skills such as copywriting need to be given special attention, and they should never be part of a bundled service that is thrown in to secure a project. As I mentioned earlier, specialized skills like writing need to be sought out with your audience rather than your bank account in mind.

We worked on a strategy and decided that the Indian firm he was working with would continue to handle tech-driven tasks like SEO and web development while graphic design work would now go to a full-time VA in the Philippines. Anything related to copywriting and product design would come back to the United States to be handled by people who truly understood his customer base.

When you're looking to outsource work, always ask yourself the following questions:

- Will this decision affect my relationship with my audience and customers?
- Is this decision motivated by cost or by the results I want to achieve?

Once you answer these two questions, a clear picture should emerge pretty quickly. You may realize that some skills and roles shouldn't be sent overseas. Keeping jobs closer to home may allow you to take care of your customers better and to provide a better overall customer experience.

As the CEO of a large company with more than 200 employees, I can personally attest to the fact that every dollar counts. However, I've also learned that sometimes being too focused on saving can end up costing me in the long run.

As I mentioned, I have VAs in the United States whom I use for specific tasks for that very reason. Outsourcing doesn't always have to equal going overseas. In my case, living in the Philippines allows me to outsource overseas to the United States, which is not something that I come across all that much, so it feels more rewarding when I do so.

What About Customer Support?

Sending customer service support overseas is a kneejerk reaction for many business owners. This is fine as long as you're dealing with a simple product or service that can be addressed by having your VA reference an FAQ sheet as he or she replies to support tickets, chat requests, and e-mail inquiries. But when it comes to expensive services—or if your brand is built on VIP-style treatment—it may not be in your best interest to service domestic customers through an overseas call center.

This is not due to a lack of education or an inability to follow direction. As I mentioned, a good VA will do everything in his or her power to please you. But when consumers of high-end products and services call support lines, they're looking for treatment that feels customized, empathetic, and confident.

Your VA may have empathy for your customers, but he or she will only be as good as the protocols you've set up. This means that your VA will need to be systematic in his or her approach to solve the customer's problem. There's nothing inherently wrong with this, but as we all know, high-end customers don't just want their problems solved. They want to feel special, too. It takes a certain mindset and cultural background to initiate meaningful small talk that makes the customer feel valued.

With a call center located in Las Vegas, Nevada, Zappos is the perfect example of an online retailer that makes its customers feel special. When I visited their facility a few years ago, I was amazed with the Zappos company culture. Everything is focused around making sure they deliver a "Wow!" to their customers during every interaction. This commitment to service even extends to the point where a representative may spend an hour on an unscripted call with a customer, helping him or her to find shoes from a competitor's website if Zappos is out of stock. The company does all of this with the knowledge that their customers will have great experiences with them, tell their friends, and eventually come back to spend money.

This type of long-form, unscripted, customer-centric phone call just isn't possible with an overseas call center. That being said—there's a series of islands in the Asian Pacific that you should focus on if you're looking for a destination where the determination to please is paramount or when there are other skill sets required from your virtual workers.

The Outsourcing
Destination of Choice: The Philippines

My company, Virtual Staff Finder, is located in Cebu City, the city with the second-highest GDP in the Philippines. Cebu City is affectionately known as the Queen City of the South and is approximately one hour south of Manila, the country's capital, via domestic airline. I've spent thirteen years living in the Philippines, so I can tell you from experience that the Filipino people are terrific. It's been a joy for my family and me to live here.

Because of the friendly nature of the Filipinos, the commitment to hard work, as well as the level of loyalty to employers, the Philippines is, simply put, the overseas destination of choice when it comes to outsourcing from the United States and other English-speaking countries, in every area from customer service to outbound lead generation to online marketing to web design and development.

Following the Spanish-American War in 1898, the Philippines became a territory of the United States when Spain gave the land to the United States for $20 million. Japan took over the country from 1942 to 1944, until the United States regained control in 1945 and granted the Filipino people full independence in 1946.

I share this history because it gives you an insight into the influences that have shaped the Filipino people, their culture, the way they live life, and the values they have toward independence.

Culturally speaking, the country is heavily influenced by Western pop culture, and many Filipino people enjoy staying current with the latest trends and celebrity icons. However, the Westernized mentalities of liberal thinking and "being your own boss" are not as common in the Philippines as they are in places like Los Angeles and Silicon Valley.

With a population of 92 million people, the Philippines is the twelfth-most populated country in the world and the world's third-largest English-speaking country. The country is 90 percent Christian with a majority of those people following the Catholic faith.

As an economy, the Philippines is new to industrialization—

which means it is transitioning from an agricultural society to one based on services and manufacturing. By 2050, it is estimated that the Philippines will have the fourteenth-largest economy in the world. So what makes the Philippines such as excellent choice for outsourcing?

The country has a long-established history of providing amazing customer service at a local level, which easily translates to providing excellent customer service on a larger scale. Huge multinationals have set up entire armies of workers in the Philippines to handle inquiries and support for customers based in the United States, the United Kingdom, and Australia. When it comes to "voice," businesses in English-speaking countries around the world turn to the Philippines for outsourced support.

When you couple this commitment to customer service with the gadget-hungry, tech-savvy mindsets of Generation Y—the twenty-somethings who will one day run the country!—you get a combination of skill sets and attitudes that make some of the best virtual employees in the world.

In the Philippines, for the most part, you're working with people who enjoy Western culture but have a strong work ethic and value secure employment, over the risks of entrepreneurship. You also tend to be working with people who are deeply grounded in their religious beliefs and thus strive to be honest and maintain their reputations. Your VA will likely be the main source of income for his or her household (most families have a single breadwinner) and will want to please you in order to keep his or her income safe and sound.

CASE STUDY #6

Fiona Lewis, E-Commerce Business Owner
Super Savvy Business

Fiona Lewis began her career as an Internet marketer in 2008. Just a few short years later in 2012, she took the knowledge she had gained and launched MumPreneursOnline.com, a website designed to give mothers a roadmap for starting online businesses from home. That same year, Fiona published her first book, *Mumpreneurs Online: Exposed*, and also launched her first membership training website—Mentoring Mums Online.

It didn't take long for Fiona to recognize a common theme that continued to surface. As an entrepreneur, she was too busy to maintain a constant, cutting-edge online presence. The demands of her growing business and Fiona's dedication to client satisfaction were becoming overwhelming tasks that left little room for everything else that needed to get done.

Something needed to change.

Why Virtual Staffing?

SuperSavvyBusiness.com was born as a result of Fiona's realization. The website had just one objective: to help overworked entrepreneurs develop cutting-edge online presences.

When she started her business back in 2008, Fiona quickly realized that she needed two of herself to keep everything in order and running properly. She constantly got caught up doing tasks that could and should have been handled by someone else. This prevented her from completely focusing on the moneymaking aspect of her business. That's when Fiona began to consider a "secret" practice that other successful marketers were using to their advantage—working with virtual assistants.

Nearly everyone around Fiona in the Internet marketing world was already outsourcing, so the transition only seemed natural for a businesswoman who needed a solution to an overworked schedule. The fact that her business was still in the early phases of development and a little strapped for funds only made it more practical to hire from overseas.

Fiona's Hurdles

There are many potential pitfalls in the world of offshore outsourcing. As a novice in this area, Fiona was unaware of how little she knew about the journey she was about to embark on.

Fiona jumped straight into the world of outsourcing without any direction or guidance from peers or mentors, so the school of hard knocks became her first teacher. She ended up spending more money than she would have liked during her learning process because she didn't understand how to manage people at an arm's length and subsequently lost a few of her first employees.

However, through tenacity and a natural savvy for business, Fiona overcame her hurdles. This list of helpful tips only proves how far she has come.

Fiona's Best Practices

- **Look for skills *and* personal values.** In the early days, Fiona was focused on hiring a person based on his or her skill sets, failing to realize that skills alone are not enough. She eventually learned that even if someone has all the skills you're looking for in a virtual worker, that person might not be the best fit for your business if he or she lacks personal values that you hold in high esteem like integrity, punctuality, and organization.

- **Look for gold—and understand its value.** When you recognize genuine talent in one of your virtual staff members, do whatever you can to keep that person. Whether you offer additional financial incentives or advancements within your organization, do everything you can to hold onto a talented, valued worker.

- **Use an outsourcing agency for roles you're unfamiliar with.** Save yourself a world of headaches and regret and hire a professional outsourcing agency to source and test candidates for you. A handful are mentioned in the Resources section of this book.

- **Hold consistent face-to-face meetings.** Thanks to Google Hangouts, Fiona's team meets every Monday. She is based in Australia and her virtual team is based in the Philippines, but there is no problem with time zones, as the two countries only have a couple of hours' time difference between them. They follow an agenda that is posted prior to the meeting so that everyone on the team knows which topics will be covered. These team meetings are not only important from a productivity standpoint, but they also build an invaluable sense of team unity. It's the only time Fiona's staff of full-time VAs can get together—and simple communication strategies make a huge difference for team morale.

- **Create ninety-day action plans.** At the beginning of each quarter, Fiona shares a ninety-day action plan with her team in order to align each person's goals and visions with the direction of the business. Each team member is then required to draw up his or her own ninety-day action plan that identifies the five main tasks he or she must focus on to drive the business forward. This allows each member to take initiative in driving his or her side of the business forward, and it truly makes success a team effort.

- **Offer training opportunities.** Each team member gets the opportunity to receive training in a specific area that supports the business and the employee's current ninety-day plan. This is a very important element of leading and developing the team. Fiona pays her VAs as they train, and the VA then benefits personally from professional growth, while the business benefits from a well-trained employee going forward.

Fiona's Tools of the Trade

Here are some of Fiona's favorite tools to use when working with her staff:

- **Google Drive** (Google.com/drive): With this cloud-storage service, all documents are stored in the same location, so there's only one up-to-date version that can be easily shared with and modified by as many people as needed. But the most powerful benefit of using Google Drive is the ability to collaborate on a document in real-time with anyone, anywhere. It's the perfect tool for a globally functioning business.

- **Google Hangouts** (Google.com/hangouts): Similar to Skype, Google Hangouts allows you to video chat with up to ten people, while also making it easy for everyone on the call to work simultaneously on a Google Drive document. This is truly multitasking at its finest!

- **Google Sites** (Google.com/sites): This cloud-based application essentially allows you to create a business intranet for you and your team to record all your systems and processes. Your only limit is your imagination.

- **Snagit** (Techsmith.com/Snagit): If you share Fiona's philosophy of systemizing each and every process within your business, it is essential to have tools that allow you to create these systems easily. Snagit is a fabulous screen capture tool that allows you to grab an image or video of what you see on your computer screen, add effects, and then share it with anyone.

Although her staff is dispersed throughout more than one country, Fiona has managed to create a unified community using these simple management tips and tools. But the ultimate reason for her success lies in the people of Super Savvy Business. Fiona says, "There's absolutely no way I would have been able to build my business as quickly and efficiently if it had not been for my virtual staff."

5 Things to Remember
When Working with Filipino VAs

One of the biggest stumbling blocks that entrepreneurs encounter when working with Filipino VAs is with the traditions and culture that affect the way their VAs do business. You must make it your business to understand the cultural and social influences guiding your VA's thought processes. I put this list together to help you and your VA get on the same page. Keep these five things in mind when working with your Filipino VA, and you'll both stay productive.

1. Filipinos Choose to Be VAs to Support Their Families

Most Filipinos don't decide to become VAs because they want to be entrepreneurs or because they dream of being their own bosses. They make the decision in order to support their families and to put others through school.

They run tight budgets and have likely already allocated the money you've promised them. That means that if you fail to pay your VAs on time, you're significantly impacting their lives. It may not seem like a lot of money to you, but that paycheck is your VA's livelihood.

Even if your business is struggling financially, always make sure that paying your VAs on time is at the top of your priority list. The last thing you want is to have a dependable VA lose trust in you and start looking for work with someone else's team.

2. Most Filipinos Live with Their Extended Families

Even if they have kids or families of their own, most Filipinos still live with their parents. You can expect a household full of kids, cousins, and sometimes aunts and uncles. This should be okay as long as it does not affect your VA's productivity.

Home-based virtual assistants should always have proper workstations and dependable Internet connections, as well as designated places to work in their homes. Preferably, your VA will have an entire room, but a small area for a computer and desk space will suffice. I would recommend asking about your VA's family to build rapport and to make sure that he or she has an adequate workspace. This will help to set the right tone for your relationship and can begin as early on as during the interview process. Filipinos love talking about their families, so don't be concerned about coming across as rude. Just ask!

3. Filipinos Do Not Like Confrontation

The Filipino people will avoid confrontations at all costs. They will probably quietly accept late payments, avoiding voicing any disagreement with the direction you're taking on a project, and listen to outbursts from you without saying anything—though they'll actually take these rants quite personally and probably think that they did something to upset you.

Take note of the language and tone you're using when communicating with your VAs over Skype. Also be careful of using ALL CAPS (which can be interpreted as shouting) in your e-mails, particularly when you're pointing out a mistake your VA made. It's not uncommon for Filipino VAs to take this sort of thing personally, and hurt feelings and bottled-up resentment ultimately lead to decreased productivity.

4. Filipinos Are Traditional

Filipinos deeply value their traditions and will not put work before important holidays. Since most of the country is Catholic, you should have a good idea of which holidays I'm talking about, and I've included them on the next page. You should take note of any special family events or cultural holidays that your VA might want to celebrate—the dates of these may change from time to time; you'll find your VA will bring them to your attention, as and when they crop up.

Here are the holidays your VA is likely to observe. Keep these dates in mind when planning large projects—and if your VA is working for you full-time, I strongly suggest giving him or her these paid days off:

- January 1—New Years Day
- April 9—Araw ng Kagitingan or Day of Valor
- May 1—Labor Day
- June 12—Independence Day
- last Sunday of August—National Heroes' Day
- November 1—All Saints' Day
- November 30—Andrés Bonifacio Day
- December 25—Christmas Day
- December 30—Rizal Day
- December 31—Last Day of the Year

These are special nonworking days declared by the Philippine government:

- Maundy Thursday (the day before Good Friday)
- Good Friday
- August 23 or any day nearest August 31st—Ninoy Aquino Day
- December 24 (a special nonworking day)

Another way of structuring the holiday setup is to take a slightly firmer approach by letting your workers know that, "I'm the boss, and this is how we're gonna do this!" Often, I suggest to clients that they set things up so that their VAs work to the clients' calendars. This means that, in the case of a US-based company, when it's a holiday in the United States, the VA in the Philippines will also have the day off—even if it's not a local holiday in the Philippines.

However, if it comes about that there is a local holiday in the Philippines but not in the United States, the VA will work through the holiday.

For the most part, this will work out fine. However, I do suggest you bend your own rules a little when it comes to religious holidays. As a general rule of thumb, you shouldn't mess with religious observances.

5. Cash Is the Best Gift—and Your VAs Will Be Extremely Grateful

Giving a physical gift is a great gesture to show appreciation for someone and what he or she does. But if you want to offer a gift to your Filipino VA, send cash (either as an additional amount with their salary, or through Western Union, as a surprise). Don't worry—it won't seem tacky or lazy. In fact, it will make a huge impact in the VA's attitude toward you and your business.

Things like home repairs are often not accounted for in your VA's monthly budget, so he or she may rely on extra surges of cash to pay for such expenses. When you give a cash gift, you're helping your VA's family out, which makes a larger impact than giving a gadget or gift card. In fact, the Filipinos have a saying for this—*utang na loob*, which means "debt of gratitude."

When you give an unexpected gift, your VA might feel like he or she owes you one. Though that isn't what you intended, it's likely to happen, so don't decline anything extra your VA wants to do for you. Just view it as part of the circle of giving.

CASE STUDY #7

Paul Holland, Online Entrepreneur
VideoTise

After twelve years of working in the film and television industry, Paul Holland became disillusioned and dissatisfied with the direction his career had taken. Not only was he discontented, but he also found himself working late nights and weekends on projects he didn't believe in. It was killing his passion for the work he had once loved.

Paul decided to pack up his life in New Zealand and head to the beautiful Gold Coast in Queensland, Australia, with just one mission: to dedicate himself to a new and satisfying venture.

He spent the next four years struggling as a small business owner until he finally decided to get back to the basics and return to the work he once loved—video. However, Paul intended to do things on his own terms this time, so he started his own business. His timing couldn't have been better because the world was just then being introduced to a platform called YouTube.

Even though most online business owners—and a few brick-and-mortar business owners—will admit that they should be using video as a means of marketing, most people don't know how to produce a video that simultaneously garners attention and generates sales. That's where Paul's company, VideoTise, comes in.

By 2011, things had really picked up and VideoTise was gaining a stronger demand for graphics-based work. This was around the time animated informational videos were gaining popularity, and Paul needed to bring on additional help to fill demand. He then faced the dilemma of whether he should hire someone from overseas or stay local.

Why Virtual Staffing?

Paul knew the style of work he was looking for and found that overseas animators were just as talented as anyone he could have found locally. And when he considered that outsourcing would cost only a fraction of what it would take to hire a local worker, the decision was clear: Paul would hire overseas.

"The impact of having a virtual staff has been amazing for my business," Paul said. "It has allowed me to take on more work than I would have if I was still working on my own and allowed me to focus on the other important stuff in the business—the sales and marketing—which then generates more work."

Outsourcing can sometimes create local jobs, which has happened in Paul's case. Since his team of VAs allowed him to focus on the sales and marketing sides of his business, he has been able to generate enough work and revenue to hire domestically.

The fantastic freedom that comes with a well-staffed, highly functioning small business is no small part of why Paul turned to virtual workers. Just recently, Paul and his wife were able to take a cruise and vacations to Fiji and New Zealand. While another business owner might fear a lapse in productivity during his or her absence, it was business as usual at VideoTise. Paul's team was able to easily stay on top of tasks he uploaded to Mindjet, a project-management tool.

Paul's Hurdles

The process of interviewing and selecting a VA was the biggest hurdle Paul faced during his virtual staffing journey. The task of going through résumés and portfolios quickly became an overwhelming project in itself. This, coupled with the horror stories Paul heard over the years about outsourcing, originally made him cautious to move forward with a virtual team.

Paul overcame his trepidation about hiring by relying heavily on online resources. He received some solid advice via blogs and other online mediums about the questions to ask and the qualities he should look for in prospective employees. However, in hindsight, Paul says he should have used an outsourcing service to "do the hard yards" as it simply took him too much time to go through all the applications, interview candidates, and finally get around to hiring.

Today, Paul has three VAs based in the Philippines—a general virtual assistant and two video and graphic editors who are helping to grow VideoTise even further.

Paul's Best Practices

- **Treat your virtual staff like in-house employees.** Though your team is based remotely, you shouldn't treat them any differently than you would treat employees working in your own office back home. This means that it's important to celebrate birthdays and to recognize special achievements. The small things really do go a long way. Paul recalls that when one of his employees had a monitor blow up, he sent $100 as a contribution toward the purchase of a new one. Though $100 doesn't seem like much, it was the equivalent of 50 percent of the employee's normal weekly wage.

- **Throw a pizza party.** As a fun and relaxed way of showing your staff you care, Paul suggests throwing a pizza party. From time to time, Paul will send a little extra money to his VAs and then has everyone hop on a group Skype chat to just talk and hang out. There's nothing like a mid-week pizza party to keep your staff motivated.

- **If you're going to call your staff a team, act like one.** If you're going to call yourselves a team, then you better do everything you can to act like one. Paul summed it up best when he said, "The point is to include them and make them feel like part of the team, and they will reward you with loyalty and hard work."

Paul's Tools of the Trade

Here are the top three tools Paul uses on a daily basis with his VAs:

- **Skype** (Skype.com): This video-calling program is a fairly recognizable household name these days. To leverage the full benefits of Skype, Paul recommends signing up for a premium account. It's inexpensive and allows for conference calls with multiple parties at once—a must-have for a globally dispersed company.

- **Mindjet** (MindJet.com): No matter which project-management system you choose to use, it is an essential tool, says Paul. He's currently using Mindjet, and it's made a significant impact on his business. He no longer worries about important e-mails disappearing in cluttered inboxes. The system is especially beneficial for Paul because his business relies heavily on editing and a substantial amount of correspondence and cooperation has to take place to complete each project.

- **Jing** (Techsmith.com/Jing): Experience has taught Paul that his VAs learn much faster if they can see a task taking place instead of just reading about it. This is why he now uses screen capture technology to give his VAs visual examples of what he's looking for. He's also found that providing these videos has allowed him to create a training library that he can reference for future projects and use to train new VAs.

Paul's virtual team is essential to the growth of his business, and he understands the ultimate benefits that come from making a conscious effort to nurture synergy and loyalty. He's already planning the launch of a new product that he sees as another fantastic opportunity for his team to grow together.

THE BIG QUESTION: STAY LOCAL OR GO OVERSEAS?

Long after this book has come and gone, the outsourcing debate between hiring local or overseas workers will continue to rage on.

As a small business owner, it's important to keep factors like business culture compatibility, location logistics, and price in mind as you decide whether to outsource work to domestic or overseas staff. Also remember that a commitment to quality should be your focus rather than trying to do what is right or wrong in the opinion of the so-called experts.

When you look at where you're standing now and where you want to stand in the future, the right option is the one that is best for your company and your customers. Making decisions based on what you read in the press or what friends are telling you to do is wrong. Ultimately, no matter where you find your VAs, capitalizing on world-class talent is what really matters.

The Next Level:
Building Your Virtual Team

Building an effective virtual team is a skill that takes time and trial and error to master, but it's definitely a skill worth acquiring. Skills are assets, and even though it may initially seem like you're putting more work into your VA program than you're getting out of it, don't worry. Your hard work will pay off.

Before we get into building your team, let's do a quick recap of the most fundamental principle in virtual staffing—thinking in terms of roles rather than tasks. The task mentality will keep you stuck on the endless merry-go-round of hiring VAs from virtual platforms like oDesk and Elance, returning each time you have another job to be done. The last place you want to be is caught in the time-consuming and exhausting freelance-hunting cycle: incessantly writing job postings, receiving small floods of response e-mails (just one job ad can generate dozens or even hundreds of responses), and taking chances on new workers before starting all over again.

When hiring, you also need to think in terms of team-building, which means looking for people who will become long-term assets to your organization.

In this section, we're going to zoom in on the concepts of building a team of virtual staff members—revisting the different types of virtual workers described in Section 1 in more detail—and what that can do for your business. We'll be handling topics such as

- cultivating a well-oiled team (hiring, moving from part- to full-time, and integrating new employees)
- the importance of setting company goals
- why you should consider meeting your virtual staff in person
- creating a social network for your VAs to use regularly
- the virtual project manager role

We'll begin with a look at how you can integrate each type of VA role into your team in order to develop a productivity engine and to create the level of freedom that we've been talking about.

How Different Types of Virtual Employees Will Work Together

Every VA is like a specialized tool, but not all jobs require the same tools. This is why it's important to understand each role individually as well as how it will function as part of a team.

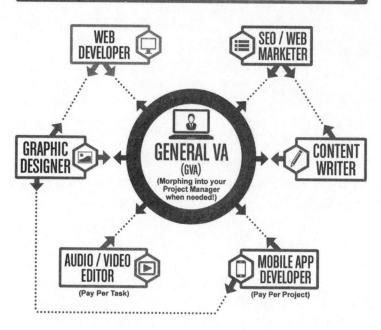

Let's break your team down into the primary VA roles I laid out in Section 1:

- general virtual assistant (GVA)
- web developer
- graphic designer
- SEO/web marketing VA
- content writer
- audio/video editor
- app developer

As always, we'll start with the GVA.

General Virtual Assistant (GVA)

Remember, this is the one type of virtual assistant that every entrepreneur on the planet should be working with. The time that these little superstars will save you is worth their weight in gold.

Tips on Hiring Someone for This Role

Finding a quality GVA is worth the wait. Typically, the best ones I've seen are moms who are looking to supplement their families' incomes while working from home.

- Use lots of bullet points in the job posting and list every task the candidate can expect to do on a regular basis.
- Use a 30-day trial period to see if the person is a fit. Don't force yourself to work with someone you have trouble communicating with. You and your GVA should have a natural and enjoyable relationship.
- If you prefer working with someone in the same time zone, whom you can call with tasks instead of e-mailing, I suggest checking out Craigslist (Craigslist.org). You'll pay more for a domestic GVA than you would for an overseas employee, but you'll have a great shot at finding someone local, for example, who was once a career professional and is now taking a different course with his or her life.

When to Make the Transition to Full-Time

If you don't feel you need someone full-time, then I recommend starting off on a part-time basis with ten to twenty hours per week so that you can get used to working with your new GVA and evaluate whether or not the position is a good fit. This role will organically transition into a full-time spot as you give the GVA more work. Remember your 3 Lists to Freedom? Go back and spend a little more time developing them—it'll help!

The real secret to using a GVA effectively is to never do work that he or she should be doing. Always ask yourself, "Is this a task I should be doing, or could I pass it along to my GVA?"

Fitting This Role into Your Virtual Team

The GVA is a unique position since his or her work is meant to assist you and doesn't fall into a specific category. However, the GVA can also operate as a type of project manager. For example, say you have two VAs working on a project to create an e-book. The project involves a content writer who will write the e-book and a graphic designer who will format the content and create a cover.

Before starting the project, you could ask your GVA to research the bestselling books on Amazon on your topic. In the same e-mail, ask him or her to message your SEO VA to begin keyword research on a specific topic that points toward current trends. Your GVA would then be responsible for returning a single e-mail to you that includes a list of links to popular Amazon books and keyword analysis to help you write an outline and market the e-book.

Once you've decided which direction you want to take, your GVA can e-mail the content writer with your notes about the topic and the outline you'd like him or her to follow. The GVA can also e-mail your graphic designer with the title of the book and links to bestselling books in the category. The graphic designer's goal is to make something comparable to other bestsellers in the category without copying anything.

That's just one example. As you incorporate your GVA into the picture over time, you can create systems that begin with a simple e-mail to your GVA and result in completed work landing in your inbox. It's pretty exciting stuff.

Web Developer

If you're like me, you know nothing about web development beyond which websites look and feel good and which ones are utter messes. I'm fine with this, and you should be, too. After all, we're business owners—not web developers.

Tips on Hiring Someone for This Role

The hardest part of hiring a web developer is that you might not know which coding skills are needed to complete the project you have in mind. If you want someone to build a simple website, that's easy. You can quickly find someone on a freelance site like Elance or oDesk to customize a WordPress site. This requires knowledge of PHP coding and—depending on the number of pages you need and how much customization you want—could cost anywhere between $50 and $500.

However, let's say you want to create something more

complex like a dating site. First, you'll need to find three to five examples of existing sites that have the functionality you want. Then you can post an ad on a job-posting site or complete a job description document with a recruitment agency that lists the examples and requires the following information:

- a list of skills the applicant thinks will be necessary to complete the project
- two examples of similar projects the candidate has completed in the past
- the candidate's most competitive bid or monthly salary option
- any suggestions the candidate has after learning a little about your project (I love doing this because it gets people thinking about working for you before they've actually been hired)

From there, you should be able to make an educated guess as to whom you should work with.

When to Make the Transition to Full-Time

Most virtual bosses don't know how to code, so working with a web developer might not be as simple as working with someone in another role. Depending on your business model, you may only need a web developer on a project-by-project basis. For this reason, you might work with a developer only when he or she builds a new site for you or makes updates to your existing website.

If you do need a full-time developer, it will quickly become apparent. But there's a catch. The developer you've been using on a project-by-project basis may not want to or be able to become a full-time member of your team, which means you'll need to hire someone from scratch. That being said, you should always ask—it's better to do so and potentially get the developer on your team than to find out that he or she took a full-time position with someone who did ask!

Fitting This Role into Your Virtual Team

The web developer will ultimately take direction from you. However, the developer should also be speaking with your graphic designer on a regular basis in order to give him or her dimensions for graphics, banners, and any other custom work that might be necessary to complete the project.

Graphic Designer

As with a web developer, you might not need a full-time graphic designer right away. However, if you're developing an online business model that will eventually turn into a full-time Internet-based business, the chances are good that at some point you'll need a permanent graphic designer on your team.

Tips on Hiring Someone for This Role

This role can be expensive domestically, but you'll be surprised by the talent and pricing you can find when you venture overseas. Keep the following tips in mind:

- Ask for a portfolio with examples of past work and run a few test projects to see if the designer is able to create the same look you're after.

- Infographics are all the rage nowadays, and a lot can be said for a graphics person who can put together a highly creative and actionable infographic. Throw one into the mix to see if your candidate is capable.
- Be sure that the person you're hiring to handle your design work already has all of the relevant software needed to do so. Software prices can be a little scary, and you shouldn't have to pay for the programs your designer is using right out of the gate. It's better to find someone who has already invested in the necessary tools to do the work.

When to Make the Transition to Full-Time

Unless you need graphic work created on a regular basis, this is the type of role that will rarely move to a full-time position. However, if regular graphic work is required, then a full-time designer is something you should seriously consider—even if your team member will have a few quiet days from time to time.

As I've become more and more active online, I recently decided to take the plunge and hired my first full-time graphic designer. So far, it's been a great decision—but if I had done it even six months earlier, it would have been too soon.

Fitting This Role into Your Virtual Team

As I mentioned earlier, I recommend connecting your graphic designer with your web developer so that your developer has the freedom to request images, icons, and buttons directly.

I should also add that if you already have someone in one of these roles and you're looking to fill the other, ask your VA to get involved in the recruiting phase for the next team member. This gives your existing employee a little pat on the back and shows that his or her input is appreciated and valued. Since the web developer and graphic designer will be working so closely together, it makes sense to have one VA help you find the other. However, involving a VA too much in the hiring decision could be detrimental to the business. He or she is your employee, not your partner—don't forget that. By all means, open the door to this type of responsibility, but be sure you have the final say. You wouldn't want your VA to ultimately veto the candidate you feel is best suited for the role and the company.

There are a lot of moving parts in the relationship between developer and designer, so you might want to monitor how they are working together in the beginning. I suggest using a project-management system to kick things off so that you can pop in and see how things are going. After a project or two, they'll probably prefer to switch to e-mail and Dropbox to share files and ideas.

SEO/Internet Marketing VA

Most small business owners are not fluent in SEO. I know I wasn't when I first started becoming active online. However, with a little reading and self-education, it's a simple enough subject that you can get a general grasp on it. The most basic thing you need to know is that your SEO VA will help you optimize your website and get it listed at the top of searches with Google and other major search engines.

Tips on Hiring Someone for This Role

Once you start interviewing, be sure to ask candidates for portfolios of sites that they've already worked on and optimized.

- Hop over to Google and type in a few relevant keywords to check out how well the candidate's websites rank. For example, if he or she optimized a website for a skateboard store in LA, you'd search for "skateboard stores in LA" and see where the website ranked in the results.
- If the candidate has been at this for a while, he or she will undoubtedly have reports to send you that show the improvement of some primary and secondary keywords he or she has worked on.
- The world of SEO changes quickly. You must insist on knowing what candidates have done to keep themselves updated with changes in the market and industry.

When to Make the Transition to Full-Time

When you start focusing more and more on the growth of the online side of your business, it's probably a good time to look into hiring a full-time SEO virtual staff member.

This marketing strategy should be seen as the online equivalent of a plumber advertising in a local newspaper—he or she advertises regularly to keep the inquiries coming in. Once you've started optimizing your website, you have to continue. Every change you make to your site has implications for SEO, and even if you make no changes at all, the search-engine industry is in an almost constant state of evolution. Simply put, if you stop focusing on SEO, your traffic will decrease and your leads will start to drop. Before you get started with SEO, you should know that it's an ongoing marketing strategy.

Fitting This Role into Your Virtual Team

This member of your team will work closely with your content writer. The SEO VA will perform initial keyword research on your industry, identify relevant search terms that will bring in the most traffic, and then pass those lists on to your content writer. Your content writer will then forward any copy he or she writes to you or your project manager (who we'll get to shortly!) for final approval. Then, the content writer will pass the work on to your web developer to post on your website.

Your SEO VA might also work regularly with your general VA on marketing concepts for YouTube videos and other types of online content.

Content Writer

When it comes to a full-time content writer, you need to make sure that this hire is a really solid one. Writing full-time is an art, plain and simple. If someone is going to be producing written content for you on a daily basis, he or she needs to be passionate about your business and your industry. Your content writer must also have the ability to self-motivate—a quality that you should really be looking for in every team member!

Tips on Hiring Someone for This Role

Whether you choose to hire an overseas or domestic content writer, I recommend that you follow these tips:

- Ask for three samples of the candidate's work and ask yourself, "Is this easy to read?" and "Would this style connect with the audience I'm trying to reach?"
- Ask the candidate to write 300 words about a recent movie he or she saw and to explain why you should watch it. This simple activity will allow you to see his or her writing abilities with regard to description and persuasion.
- Keep an eye out for anyone who overuses big words in an effort to sound smart. You won't find too many in this book, I assure you!

Here's a quick bonus tip in case you do end up hiring someone from overseas: if you're working on a large project together like an e-book or a collection of web articles that will be used to market one of your online products, hire someone domestically to proofread the writing before it goes live. This person can clean up the content writer's work by smoothing out any areas that sound forced—and it will likely be a lot cheaper than hiring a domestic writer. This setup gives you the best of both worlds and is one that I incorporate regularly on my marketing materials.

When to Make the Transition to Full-Time

If your business model consists of reaching across multiple niches and selling info products online, then you need a full-time content writer ASAP.

Even if that isn't your business model, I suggest bringing on a writer or editor to review your work each month. Some entrepreneurs feel that typos and simple grammar issues aren't worth the trouble (or cost) of hiring someone to check for them, but I disagree—especially if you're trying to build a reputation in your industry. Your potential clients are looking for reasons to not trust you. Why give them any?

Fitting This Role into Your Virtual Team

Here's my suggested workflow for content writers:

Step 1: Your writer receives a Google Drive document with a set number of monthly topics and due dates researched by you or someone on your team, such as your SEO VA or GVA.

Step 2: Your writer sends the finished articles to your GVA, who then uploads the writing and any accompanying images to whichever websites they'll be published on. They go live following your approval.

Step 3: Your GVA updates the Google Drive document you've created that lists each month's topics and due dates, stating that they have been, or will soon be "published". If your writer is late in delivering the article, your GVA sends an e-mail to him or her and copies you in.

Video Editor

There are plenty of editing tools online, such as Animoto (Animoto.com), that allow you to create engaging videos for free. You can also purchase the premium versions of these tools to get additional resources and to produce longer videos. These are fun tools to use, but be careful about getting sucked into doing your own video editing. You could easily spend an entire day editing a three-minute video. You might have a lot of fun doing it, but you need to remember that as the boss, your time is better used elsewhere.

Tips on Hiring Someone for This Role

Hiring a video editor has nothing to do with the candidates' résumés or where they went to school. Your decision should be entirely based on the completed work they have produced. Either the candidates have it or they don't! Keep the following tips in mind:

- Always ask for access to the candidate's demo reel.
- See if the candidate's work matches the style you're looking for. It does you no good to hire an amazing editor who works on short films if you're looking for someone to animate text for your online videos.
- If you take the job-posting route for this position, you're going to get a huge response. I suggest having someone else like your GVA or project manager go through all of the proposals and weed out any editors who did not submit an example of their work or do not have any examples that match the style you want.
- Find an editor to work with directly, instead of choosing someone from an agency that has a lot

of editors on staff. This will allow you to form a direct relationship with the video editor that can be developed in the future.

- Look for someone who's already invested his or her own time and money into developing the editing skills you want. This level of commitment is a great trait for this type of role.

When to Make the Transition to Full-Time

This will depend solely on the amount of video you want to incorporate in your business strategy. Keep in mind that it takes a lot longer to edit a video than to create a storyboard, produce a script, and shoot it. Even if your video editor is only cutting three or four videos a month, it's going to keep him or her pretty busy.

There really is no rule of thumb to determine when you should transition your video editor from a project basis to part time to full time. Typically the editor's hours will simply increase organically.

I recommend working with more than one video editor. If one of the editors falls through or needs to put things on hold due to a personal or family emergency, you'll still have a backup. When you're creating video content regularly, a backup editor is a godsend—trust me, I know from experience.

Fitting This Role into Your Virtual Team

I love online video and produce a lot of it. With that in mind, I'm just going to tell you exactly how my video editor VA fits into my team.

Step 1: As the content producer, I shoot the video and then pass it onto my video VA via Dropbox.

Step 2: He edits the video following guidelines and certain standards that we've already set and then uploads a low-resolution version into Dropbox for me to review. Once I approve it, he exports the full HD version of the clip.

Step 3: Finally, my GVA picks up the video, uploads it to YouTube, embeds it into a blog post, and publishes it for the world to enjoy.

Awesome, huh? If I want to take it to the next level, my content writer transcribes the video so that I can use the text as a separate blog post, insert it into an e-book, or utilize it as a PowerPoint presentation in the future.

We're talking about creating a content repurposing machine that allows you to convert several pieces of content into many other media types. No matter what your customers prefer, there's a form of content for everyone to enjoy. We'll go into this idea in a big way in the next section. You're going to love it!

App Developer

The biggest thing to keep in mind with this role is that there's more to mobile app creation than just making the app. There's the submission of the app to an app store or directory, promotion of the app, and the uploading of new content and updated versions of the app over time.

Tips on Hiring Someone for This Role

Much like web design, you're either going to know your stuff here or not. My gut instinct is that you won't have a single idea how this gets done, just as I didn't! Making sure that the person you're thinking of hiring knows his or her stuff is one thing, but when you can actually see the work the candidate has already accomplished for other people, the proof is in the pudding.

- Make sure the candidate you're considering has at least a handful of fully designed, built, and marketed apps available to the public.
- Check into those apps. Download them—even if you have to pay for them!—and feel what the customer feels as he or she experiences the app.
- Because of its new place in the market, this is the one role where personal recommendations mean a lot. Ask around to see if you know anyone who, er, knows of anyone.

When to Make the Transition to Full-Time

In terms of virtual staffing, app creation is a project-based role unless you anticipate becoming an app-building company! Ongoing maintenance and updates can be handled on a case-by-case basis, which means you can work with one developer as needed or try out different developers at different times to get a feel for their work and perspective on the direction you should take.

Fitting This Role into Your Virtual Team

The only person your app developer will need to interact with regularly other than you is your graphic designer.

The app developer and graphic designer VAs will work together to determine how the app looks to the end user. From the wireframe that outlines how the app will work to the end product, all of the planning will need to be handled by the app developer and you or your project manager.

Lifestyle entrepreneur Lewis Howes is an ex-pro athlete turned podcaster, speaker, business coach, and content creator. He plays the delegation game perfectly. Except for his personal assistant (who works physically with him), he only hires on a project basis—but it's using the right people for the right jobs that makes what he does so effective. His VAs—whether video editors, app developers, podcast engineers, or web developers—always work together as a team. It's this focus on hiring the right people for the right roles that has catapulted Lewis to Internet marketing stardom and garnered him a massive online following.

The examples I've used in this section showing how individual members of a virtual team work together are just the beginning. I could almost write an entire book on this subject, with additional blueprints illustrating how to do this. I have produced some material on this subject as part of the Going Virtual series that you can access for free on my blog. The direct link is ChrisDucker.com/Going Virtual.

Once you've got your team in place, it's time to get everyone motivated. There's no better way to do that than to set some goals!

CASE STUDY #8

Nate Ginsburg, Digital Nomad
Onset LLC

Meet Nate Ginsburg, a self-proclaimed digital nomad.

Nate's title originated during his early beginnings as a digital entrepreneur. As he tested out some ill-fated web ideas in an effort to find a source of passive income, Nate traveled the world and gained some insightful exposure to outsourcing.

One of Nate's first clients was a cosmetic surgery site. Because he didn't know how to code and didn't have time to write all of the content, he turned to oDesk to hire people who could. With all its different features and options, the job-posting platform certainly wasn't love at first sight, but after some trial and error, it became a viable option for handling client work and developed into Nate's go-to source when he needed to get things done. Eventually, Nate's experience in identifying and hiring talented outsourcers helped him start his Internet marketing service business, OnsetLLC.com.

As a business, Onset has one objective—to implement innovative and effective Internet marketing campaigns in order to create profit centers for its clients. As the company has grown, Nate's methods for handling staffing have also evolved. He still flirts with oDesk periodically, but he has now grown his own team of virtual staff members who work for him on a regular basis in areas such as web design, web development, SEO, PPC (pay-per-click advertising), social media, and mobile app development.

Why Virtual Staffing?

Nate says, "I cannot understate the impact that working with virtual staff has had on my business. It allowed me to get started in the Internet marketing niche, and I now confidently will take on any sort of project knowing that I can find and hire top talent for anything that I am unable to accomplish myself."

The entrepreneur inside of Nate knows that he can't do everything. He's good at certain things and does continue to work on client projects personally—but it's the ability to delegate work and offload tasks that he isn't familiar with that makes virtual staffing his primary focus when it comes to handling the growth of his business.

Nate's Hurdles

The biggest hurdles Nate faced initially were fairly basic. He had trouble writing accurate job descriptions and was a little lost when it came to identifying desirable qualities in his candidates.

Nate also feels that his underdeveloped employer profile on the job-posting site was a hurdle. Employer profiles are typically designed to help VAs gauge whether or not you are a serious employer by showing your hiring history and project activity. One way to build such a history swiftly is to post and hire for a handful of small, quick-to-complete jobs, such as logo design or transcription work. Now that Nate is a seasoned employer, he has the luxury of hiring only top candidates who compete fervently for a position in his company. Nate has now hired virtual workers to manage more than 100 contracts for his business.

Nate's Best Practices

Here are a few ways Nate has used his VAs to streamline processes and leverage his time:

- **Delegate repetitive tasks.** Nate has his general VA keep tabs on roughly a dozen news publications and send him a bullet-point list of headlines each morning. This isn't a high-end task, but it was a time-consuming one that Nate was spending his own time doing.

- **Know when to grow.** One of the biggest shifts that Nate had to handle was transitioning from a team of individual freelance workers to developing his own dedicated team of full-time virtual workers on his payroll. Nate would balance workload, feelings of being overwhelmed, and how his staff was handling deadlines to assess when the next growth spurt was needed, and then act accordingly. The ability to know when to grow is important from a financial standpoint and from a business-growth angle.
- **Learn from your VAs.** Nate sometimes hires VAs with specific skills to teach him something. For example, when a client required Nate to use the Google AdWords management program, Nate hired a top AdWords expert on oDesk to go through each of his client's campaigns and give him tips on how to optimize them. This helped his client's campaigns and also accelerated his own learning curve.

Nate's Tools of the Trade

You've seen these before, and you'll see them again. Here are Nate's two go-to tools for managing his team day to day:

- **Skype** (Skype.com): Nate chats back and forth with his staff on a daily basis via Skype. He's also a fan of the tool's screen-sharing ability for when he spends time walking his VAs through new tasks.
- **Dropbox** (Dropbox.com): This file-sharing tool allows Nate's VAs to upload their writing tasks (in Word documents) to him in real time. The files automatically sync with Nate's computer and mobile devices, which allows the entire team to be on the same page.

Nate is the perfect example of an entrepreneur who utilized the power of outsourcing to grow his business and create freedom in his life simultaneously. The fact that he can continue to run and grow his business while staying on the move for extended periods of time is just awesome—and it's what virtual freedom is all about.

Setting Company Goals and Rewards

Many companies throw out the word "team" a lot during their interviewing processes, saying things like, "We operate in a team environment," or, "We're really looking for team players." That's usually just code for, "We want someone who puts the company first and does not question management."

Sorry, but that's not a team. The basic definition of a team is a group of people working toward a common goal. That's what a team truly is.

However, simply having that group of people working together is not enough if you really want to utilize them properly in your quest toward virtual freedom. As the boss, you're the one with the skills and the authority to effectively set and manage goals and targets.

You'll enjoy several key benefits when you give your team a common goal or something exciting to work toward besides the next PayPal deposits. I'll explain those benefits in more detail in just a moment, but let's first look at a few examples of team goals.

- **Set a sales goal and reward everyone on your team if you hit it.** It doesn't have to be a cash gift—the reward could be, for example, Amazon gift cards that the VAs can use on their families. Even if your VAs are not directly involved with the selling process, everyone's work contributes to the end result and they should all be rewarded.

- **Set a calendar goal for completing a project.** The project could be a revision of your website, the creation of a new product or service, or even a complete rebranding of your company's look.

- **Set loyalty benchmarks and award appropriate bonuses.** This is exactly as it sounds—a gift that rewards loyalty. Obviously, you'll want to select a gift that reflects the amount of time each team member has been with you. At our company we have yearly awards given out to all employees, along with gift certificates and cash bonuses. The longer the employee has been with us, the larger the amount of cash they receive.

Here are the aforementioned key benefits to establishing these common goals:

- It encourages loyalty.
- It shows your newer VAs that loyalty is valued.
- It reinforces the meaning of the word "team."
- Small gestures go a long way, especially in other cultures.
- It makes your VA feel like he or she is a part of something. Isn't this the kind of place you want to work?

An added benefit of encouraging loyalty through team goals

is that your next hire might be an internal referral. The next time you're looking to fill a role or complete a project, your VAs will be proud to recruit for you.

There are a few reasons why internal referrals are effective as you continue to grow your team. First, using your current staff to find new team members saves time, money, and effort in recruiting and advertising. It also allows you to have your virtual staff members take your new recruits under their wing and have a feeling of ownership attached to the growth of their fellow teammates. Finally, it creates brand loyalty within your organization—something that I believe in strongly.

Some of the best VAs you'll hire will be recommended by other VAs on your team. Just make sure to only take recommendations from your long-standing VAs. They won't want to damage their reputation with you, which means they're likely to give you quality referrals.

Meeting Everyone in Person

Before taking the leap into full-time entrepreneurship, most people sit in their offices or cubicles and daydream of the days they'll be free of pointless meetings and reporting to managers who serve up company Kool-Aid. But once that day arrives and freedom is no longer a fantasy, the entrepreneur soon realizes something—entrepreneurship is lonely.

The human interaction you once experienced during the day is now gone—and let's face it, even though the people at the office may not have been your best friends, it was nice to feel a sense of belonging.

Then there's the issue of productivity. Say two employees are working on the same project. Each of them is responsible for a different part, and they'll need to communicate on a consistent basis to complete the work. They can e-mail each other or call each other with questions or comments, but every now and then, each employee will decide to walk over to the other's desk and have a good, old-fashioned conversation instead. E-mail is great—but it can never replace face-to-face collaboration.

Unfortunately, this is where virtual staffing can fall short. Even though you may have a team of people working for you, the physical separation of your team can create a disjointed feeling for everyone involved and a bottleneck effect that leaves you as the middleperson for everyone. This is why it's essential to have your team meet on a consistent basis.

In a perfect world, that would mean getting everyone together in a meeting room where you can spend the day brainstorming with a whiteboard as people get to know one another better. If your team is separated across different time zones and continents, this may not be an option, although I do know several business owners with virtual teams in the Philippines who love to come over and spend a week or so in the sun while enjoying brainstorming minus stuffy meeting rooms!

If you have the ability to meet in person with your team on a regular basis, then I absolutely suggest you do it. If you don't, fear not—we live in the twenty-first century, and there are some fantastic tools, such as Google Hangouts, Skype, and online meeting software like GoToMeeting (GoToMeeting.com), at your disposal.

Here are a few tips for encouraging virtual interaction among your team members:

- **Introduce your team to one another for the first time.** The first step is to have your team meet one another. You can facilitate the introductions in a group chat and have each member say a few words about him- or herself. The purpose of this is to break the ice and allow each member to associate names and voices with the other people on the team instead of viewing them as e-mail addresses.

- **Encourage your team members to chat with one another.** Sometimes a problem will be resolved a lot faster through a conversation than through a series of e-mails—but it's up to you to encourage that. Don't expect a VA to reach out and chat with a member of the team he or she has never met before. This is also why it's so important to introduce everyone in the beginning!

- **Meet regularly as a team.** I'm not saying you should start having weekly meetings, but I would suggest a monthly group meeting where you can recap how things have gone in the last few weeks and discuss how you can improve as a team.

- **Talk one-on-one with your team members.** This goes deeper than sending an e-mail saying, "Need anything?" or "Keep up the great work." This tip is about connecting one-on-one with each of your team members to ask for feedback and suggestions on how things could improve. It's also a time to thank each person for his or her work and to connect with each VA on a personal level.

If your team is spread out over different time zones, then you'll need to take it in turns as to who might have to stay up late or wake up early to be involved in the meetings. Remember, you're the boss, and the time of the meeting should be convenient to you before anyone else, but do consider the other team members, too.

Everyone wants to belong to something. Creating a team atmosphere is the best way to make sure your VAs gel with one another. It will help your operation run more efficiently and remove you from the middleperson position.

Setting Up a Social Network for Your Virtual Team

Now that you've established a company culture of interaction, you may want to consider setting up your own VA social network.

A digital platform like Facebook or Yammer that allows your VAs to connect privately is a brilliant idea. This may be excessive if you only have two or three VAs, but it will serve as a good breeding ground for collaboration once you're running a team of at least five people. You can even include freelancers who were brought on for one-time projects in order to develop relationships and promote the importance of high-quality work throughout the entire team.

It's best to keep things simple here: I don't suggest hiring a web developer to build an entire platform for you from scratch. There are a few great options already out there that you can use right away, such as

- **A private Facebook group**: This is free to create and easy to get people to use because practically the entire planet is already on Facebook. Unlike other areas of the site that are mostly public, you can set up a private Facebook group where only members who have been specifically invited can see what's going on inside.

- **A LinkedIn group**: This isn't my first option, mainly because my virtual staff are not all that active on the platform—but even if you don't create a LinkedIn group for your virtual team, I recommend starting a professional group for your industry or city. It can be a great lead generation tool.

- **A Google+ Community**: You can start a G+ Community for free and then invite the members directly. Just be sure to set it up as a closed group.

- **Yammer**: This really is an enterprise social network, and I love it. Yammer.com also has brilliant mobile app versions for iPhone and iPad.

- **Ning**: You can also launch your own digital community. Depending on the number of team members, you can choose from different pricing options with Ning.com. It's a solid choice if you have a very large team.

- **BuddyPress**: This allows anyone to create a social networking site on the WordPress platform.

The main focus here is to create a team element where people feel comfortable working and chatting together online. I've had excellent success with mine—my team has used both Facebook and Yammer—and I'm sure you will, too.

How can you promote interaction without providing the means to do so? Once again, this is something you only need to consider once your team begins growing beyond five employees—otherwise there won't be too much going on!

FREEDOM SPOTLIGHT

Joe Daniel
Coaching Expert
The Football-Defense Report

Joe Daniel managed to develop his passion for coaching high-school football into an entrepreneurial venture that includes his website, Football-Defense.com, and a podcast that helps American football coaches with their schemes, practice planning, game plans, and coaching philosophies.

❯ The Problem

It wasn't long before Joe's triple life of coaching, teaching, and running his online businesses began to get a little overwhelming. Joe was spending seventy hours a week on teaching and coaching and he just didn't have time to manage the mundane tasks that were necessary to keep his website and podcast up and running.

❯ The Solution

To help solve his time-management problem, Joe hired just one virtual assistant. Joe's VA was from the Philippines and worked with him for about sixteen months, handling podcast editing, podcast transcriptions, and much of the site's online customer service. Joe was amazed at the quality of service he received from his VA and believes that it's just not as common to find such an honest and intelligent employee in the United States.

❯ The Outcome

Joe is now focused 100 percent on his passion, teaching and coaching football players and coaches—and he insists that part of the reason his system is so easy to run himself is because of how well his virtual assistant set it up. That's right. Joe has gone full-circle. However, he's no longer juggling those crazy hours and he's happier overall.

When to Create the Virtual Project Manager Role

Before we discuss the process for hiring a project manager, let's quickly recap why you began venturing down the road of virtual staffing in the first place: to free yourself from performing tasks so that you could focus on the strategy and growth of your business.

We've come a long, long way since we first got into this topic. By now, you could well be sitting pretty with several staff members on your virtual team—and if you're not already, my guess is that you will be soon enough.

In the beginning, you will always be the manager by default. Maybe it's been that way for a while or maybe you're just starting to feel it—but either way, it's time to start getting things back on track. We're ready to transition you from the role of manager to business owner. We'll do that by bringing a special someone on board to help you run things.

I'd like to wrap up this section on team building by focusing on four main components of working with a virtual project manager (VPM):

- knowing when the time is right for a VPM
- finding a VPM
- hiring a VPM
- working with a VPM

When Is a Virtual Project Manager Necessary?

The moment you begin working with at least three or four full-time members on your virtual team, you've created a need for a project manager. Whether you like it or not, that role is instantly filled by you—and will continue to be filled by you until you bring a project manager on board. For some business owners, this is exactly where they want to be—running things in the middle of it all. However, you know me by now, and you know that I'd argue that running things isn't the best use of your time!

You don't have time to be the project manager. As someone who has taken action in today's market and built a virtual team of support and marketing staff, you're already in a new role as the chief growth officer. As the CGO, your role is to continually find ways to work on the business—not in it.

This means you need to put the right people and systems into place so that you can afford the time to identify new opportunities for growth. To truly utilize the power of your team, a virtual project manager is one of the most important roles you can put into place. This is why I recommend looking to fill this important role once your team reaches a benchmark of three or four full-time employees. You won't find a project manager overnight, but you should at least start thinking about the process.

I should also point out that this benchmark is about the same time you'll begin to feel that same sense of freedom slipping away that you felt when you first began hiring virtual staff. You're not doing anything wrong. It's just the natural progression of things. Simply put:

→ **More Success and Growth = More Work = More Staff = More Management**

However, that progression doesn't—and shouldn't—mean that you need to let go of any more freedom than you're comfortable with. Freedom is still our main focus. Consider a gas tank: When your gas level starts to get low, you simply fill 'er up, right? In this case, you need to re-fuel yourself and your business by taking yourself out of the equation once again and finding someone else to come in and run the team for you.

Where to Find a Virtual Project Manager

Have you ever heard the saying, "The best jobs aren't advertised"? If you haven't before, you have now! The same is true for a VPM. The best VPMs aren't recruited—they're discovered.

One of the first people you should consider is your own general virtual assistant. In many ways, your GVA has acted as your right hand since the beginning. Your GVA has a good understanding of your processes, especially if he or she has been the middleperson who helps you coordinate the projects and tasks that keep your business running.

In fact, most VPMs were GVAs at one time or another. They evolved into their current positions by demonstrating attention to detail and by hitting deadlines consistently. My suggestion is to only consider a GVA who has been working with you full-time for at least one year—and only if he or she has demonstrated a strong sense of personal drive, leadership, and communication ability. These are the traits that will drive your GVA to go above and beyond what he or she does for you.

To see if your GVA is a good potential fit for a VPM role, begin giving him or her projects to manage. Start with something small and see how your GVA does.

A recruitment service is another avenue you can use to find a VPM. If you've grown your team quickly and you don't have a GVA who has demonstrated the necessary traits to take his or her career to the next level, a recruitment service is the perfect option. This doesn't mean you shouldn't consider your current GVA for a promotion in the future—but if you need a VPM now, then you need one now!

A recruitment partner is typically a faster way to hire someone than to post a listing on a job board. You'll obviously still need to spend some time training your new VPM on your company's procedures and policies, but the candidate's experience level should be good enough to ensure that he or she can take whatever guidance you offer and run with it.

Due to the recent trend of downsizing, there are a lot of great people out there in the global job market who are looking for freelance careers instead of a returning to a typical corporate environment. This phenomenon has been referred to as the "gig economy," with more than 42 million Americans working as self-employed consultants and freelancers. For the small- to medium-size business owner or start-up entrepreneur, this means that you can acquire talented people without having to hire them full-time or offer expensive benefits packages.

A quick look at Craigslist will give you a handful of decent options on any given day. Obviously, a US-based project manager is likely to be more expensive than an overseas VPM, but the domestic candidate's experience should allow you to get going a little faster. I wouldn't suggest you take this route to find a long-term, full-time employee unless you are willing to continue to pay a premium for the service. However, it's a great option as a quick fix or when you need to hand over a project with a fixed end date.

How to Hire a Virtual Project Manager

If you're promoting your GVA to the VPM role, you probably won't need to conduct a formal interview. However, if you're bringing someone new into the position, you need to really focus on creating an interview process that narrows your search to a few prime candidates—just as you did when you first brought your other virtual workers on board.

Don't rely on a résumé to tell you an entire story. Just because someone has already worked as a GVA or a project manager for a number of years, that doesn't automatically mean he or she is good at it—and it doesn't guarantee that the candidate will work well with you, your team, or your business.

When hiring for this particular role I like to take an unconventional step. It's something a little out of the ordinary and far removed from the typical process of e-mailing a résumé with a cover letter. Ask the VPM candidate for something that demonstrates creativity and a high attention to detail. For example, have each potential VPM draw you a picture of the best vacation destination he or she has ever visited or write you a quick paragraph about his or her favorite animal. I know it sounds a bit gimmicky, but if you place this request at the end of your job posting, you'll quickly see who was paying attention and you'll get a sense of each candidate's personality.

If you're using Skype for the interview, you should also absolutely insist on using the webcam feature of the software in addition to audio. You'll be able to get a better feel for the candidate's demeanor and see if he or she has the confidence it takes to lead a team while maintaining an approachable attitude.

As you interview VPM candidates, it's imperative that you ask them to discuss past projects they've led—both successful and unsuccessful ones. Ask them to elaborate a little on why those projects did or didn't work out. However, don't just leave it at story time—dig a little deeper.

Request information on why each candidate's project was so successful and why he or she was an important part of that success. This allows each person to sell him- or herself a little.

At some point, it's inevitable that your VPM will run into some kind of pushback or excuse from another member of the team when a task isn't completed. Ask each candidate how he or she would manage this type of conflict. The candidate's answer will allow you to see how he or she is going to handle potential internal issues.

Tips for Working with a Virtual Project Manager

Once you've identified a potential VPM, I would suggest working with the candidate on a trial basis to see how he or she does. This could be a period of time, such as ninety days or for the duration of a particular project. Even if you've decided to move your GVA up the ladder into this new role, I'd still suggest putting a trial period in place. This ensures that your GVA knows that it's important to prove himself or herself to you before getting the job for good.

Working effectively and successfully with your VPM isn't going to be a whole lot different than working with your first GVA. However, there are a few extra points that I'd like to cover:

- Your VPM will be responsible for assigning tasks to individual team members based on the project. The VPM will also set deadlines and meetings as he or she sees fit. However, it's important for your VPM to know that even though there are several different moving parts to the machine, the timely completion of the project falls squarely on his or her shoulders—no one else's.

- Empower your VPM to make a specific dollar amount of purchases each month (anything over that set amount should require approval from you.) This gives him or her a sense of ownership and also shows the rest of the team that there is someone else around who has the power to spend a little of the company's money, thus promoting a sense of hierarchy within the team.

- Even if you're a solopreneur, bring your VPM into your strategy and brainstorming sessions. He or she can help you set realistic deadlines and can be a valuable resource as you bounce ideas around. Getting your VPM involved in this side of the business is a great way to show that you trust him or her to work for you at a higher level.

- Have your VPM create an operations manual. This is the one project I think you should have your VPM handle on a consistent basis. The manual puts a standardized process in place for your organization, helping you train future VAs and even allowing you to transition them into VPMs if needed.

Building a virtual team is something that might be far from a reality for you right now. You might have picked up this book to learn how to get started with freelancers or perhaps to figure out how to get that one GVA on board. That's fine. Really.

The most important thing here is that you learn to believe in the concept of building a team of people to help you virtually run, support, and grow your business. Keep in mind that building a team is a skill that's developed over a period of time—but it is a skill that must be developed in order for you to truly grow your business. There is no reason why you can't follow in the steps of the countless entrepreneurs who are featured in this book—and no reason why you can't also take things to the next level.

Remembering to stay honest to yourself and the beliefs and dreams that led you on this journey is the single most powerful concept you can follow. The virtual freedom you're chasing down will enable you to build a great team—and in turn, your team will help you build one hell of a business!

Your team will also help to keep your feet planted firmly on the ground as you continue to produce great products, services, and content to help, educate, inspire, and entertain people. In the new world of business, it's this last piece—content—that will set you apart from your competition. Content is undoubtedly the focus for the big players in your industry—and it's a focus you need to have ASAP.

So, let's talk content.

The Case for Content

Your virtual freedom is about more than trying to work fewer hours each day, week, or month. It's about leveraging that freedom in order to create more building blocks for your business—and here in the twenty-first century, there's no better way to build your business than to create and market content online.

In this section, we'll go over the reasons you need to create online content. We'll also focus on

- producing online content consistently
- what makes "good" content
- why all online content is not created equally
- the P2P (people-to-people) philosophy
- injecting yourself into your content
- step-by-step content processes for your virtual team

Keep in mind that when I say "content," I'm not talking about boring corporate websites that use 2,000 words to outline a mission statement or a company that features a montage of *Jackass*-style stunts on YouTube.

What I'm talking about is the type of content that delivers

- a clear, concise message
- education and solutions that solve problems
- inspiration that spurs people to take action instead of focusing on entertainment

Those are a few of the qualities of good content—and good content is hard to find. These days, the first stop for almost anyone looking to solve a problem is the Internet. As providers of products or services, problem-solving is exactly what we should be focusing on. Here are just a few of the problems that drive people to the Internet to look for answers—where hopefully, once they're online, they'll discover high-quality content.

- **Health issues**: Obesity is no longer just an American problem. There are now six other countries in which 20 percent of the population is medically obese. So where do people turn when they have questions about their cholesterol or when they need advice about nutrition, exercise programs, and exercise equipment? If your business provides meal plans, workout supplies, or other solutions to health problems, people will turn to you.
- **Financial questions**: Where should a couple invest for their child's education? What should people know about identity theft? If you faced financial stress, hardship, or uncertainty, where would you turn for information to get your life

back on track? If your blog and podcast tackle these problems, people are going to start turning to you.

- **Career issues**: Where does a college graduate or recently unemployed middle manager look for work? How do people stay informed and up to date with the most desirable skills in today's marketplace? If someone is tired of the job search and wants to become an entrepreneur instead, where should he or she start? If your web show or e-mail newsletter offers tips and tactics to people in these situations, they'll be tuning in to watch you or signing up for your e-mail list.

- **Business communication questions:** How does a small, family-owned business stay relevant in a world driven by social media? How do experienced business owners communicate and connect with today's consumers? If your online courses and live workshops show them how, these small business owners will become instant fans and customers for life!

People are looking for answers, and they're looking for them right now. But what if the best answers aren't available? What if your business has the solution to someone's problem, but you haven't put it out there so that it can be found? If someone has a business that's equipped to answer common questions, shouldn't he or she have content available in the most popular place that people search for answers?

Perhaps business owners don't focus on producing

content because they lack the tools to do so. Perhaps computers, cameras, and Internet access are too hard to find. No—that doesn't seem right. Could it be cost? Maybe it simply costs too much to create quality content and market it online. No—that doesn't make sense either. Anyone can create a YouTube channel and upload a video for free. Anyone reading this book could put it down right now and publish his or her first blog post without reaching for a credit card.

So what's the problem? If it's not access, tools, or cost, then what is it?

The real problem is time. It takes time to research and write a high-quality blog post. It takes time to film and edit a YouTube video that engages audience members while also presenting a clear message and call to action. It takes time to create a powerful webinar that presents life- and business-changing information in an entertaining manner that keeps attendees from being distracted or leaving early.

I'm sure right now there's a large pool of potential content on your iPad, on your laptop, or in your head, just sitting there and waiting to be sorted out, produced, published, and released into the digital world.

Consider how many times you have said

- "I should share one of my clients' stories as a case study."
- "I need to write a book about _____."
- "I really should shoot a YouTube video about _____."
- "This month, I'm going to create my _____."
- "I need a website."

The list goes on, and all of this amazing content is just sitting around, collecting dust and quickly becoming irrelevant when it could be out there helping people, building your brand, and making an impact. That's the reason why I'm writing this chapter and this book. I know you're busy, and I know you probably don't have time to do any of the things I listed here.

This is about helping qualified people get free from the tasks that are holding them back so they can return to the most important parts of their businesses—leading and selling.

Why Your Business Needs to Produce Online Content Consistently

When you last encountered a piece of content that made a positive impact on your personal life or business, I'm sure you were happy someone had created it. However, have you ever asked yourself what it takes to produce that type of content? As I see it there are two requirements to producing great content: experience and skill.

Part 1: The Experience

The content creator must be an expert who has had—and continues to have—consistent success in a particular area that qualifies him or her to teach. This experience could have been acquired under someone else's mentorship or it could be self-taught.

Part 2: Technical and Creative Skill

Armed with experience, the expert decides to share it. He or she might share the experience through blog posts, YouTube videos, a newsletter, or even a podcast. However, not only will the expert need an understanding of digital content creation—or a team behind him or her that does—but he or she will also need to make the content engaging and easy to follow in order to hold onto the audience's attention.

Who has time for all of that? Does an expert who's successful and presently engaged in his or her craft really have the time to produce content that entertains and instructs? Probably not. Even experts who have dedicated themselves to full-time teaching and learning can quickly become overwhelmed with the amount of work and detail that goes into researching, syndicating, and promoting content.

But people *are* searching for solutions to their problems online. I'm sure people are searching for questions right now that you could answer, so what can you do? Do you have the time to create content that can be easily found and shared?

You might have time at first, but you'll soon find that it's impossible to do all of this by yourself. No one can be his or her own production company—trust me. I've tried and failed miserably. You'll need help; that's where your team of VAs can play a vital role—assisting you in researching, producing, and marketing quality content.

I'm not talking about producing content every day, because that's excessive. Frequency is less important than producing content that's genuinely engaging and has a message that can positively impact lives. You are providing a service to those who need or want it, and it serves no one if you get burnt out because you're trying to churn out too much content.

Additionally, content—especially for the web—can (and in many cases should) be brief. People are searching online for quick solutions or answers. A solution might be as simple as a video showing how to upload a blog post to WordPress or a checklist outlining tasks you can outsource to your first virtual assistant. (You can find my personal checklist at ChrisDucker.com/101.)

Before we get into how to incorporate your VAs into the production process, let's discuss why you should consider content creation at all. We just spoke about some of the problems our world is facing today and considered that people are turning to the Internet to find solutions. That should be enough for anyone with a business in today's economy to start planning his or her content creation strategy. The simple fact is that if you're not in the digital loop, you're missing out on enormous opportunities as a business owner.

What about small, local businesses—do they still need to think about content creation? Maybe you've got a small bookkeeping company, pet day-care center, or health spa, and you're wondering why you should concern yourself with digital content.

Here are some common excuses I hear from business owners as to why they are not creating content, and my rebuttals to them:

- **My business doesn't sell products online. We want people to visit our stores to make purchases.** Did you know that 94 percent of smartphone users use their mobile devices to search for information about local businesses?

They're not looking to buy products online—they're looking for reviews, pictures, location information, and anything else that will help them decide whether or not to visit your business. Whenever I'm in the United States and looking for restaurants, hotels, or other types of local businesses, I personally do this by using Yelp's mobile app. If that's not enough to get your attention, consider this simple fact: 61 percent of local searches result in a phone call to a business.

- **We've been getting along fine for years without online content. Why start now?** Today's consumer relies on digital content and influence from online social circles to guide his or her buying decisions. How we use the Internet and how much we use it is evolving at a lightning-fast pace, especially now, with the advent of smartphones, because people take the Internet with them everywhere they go. Something like a blog post or Facebook fan page that may seem small to you can make a huge difference in the eyes of your local market. In fact, it could be the very thing that makes customers realize you exist in the first place.

- **We have die-hard customers who bring us business by referral.** Why not give these fans something digital to promote? It's a lot easier for someone to "like" the Facebook fan page of your business than to call all 300 of his or her Facebook friends.

- **We already have a website and professional video on our homepage.** That's great—but is that video also on your YouTube channel? Do you even know why that's important? What are you doing to make it easier for customers to find this website of yours? Are you using the website as a lead-generation device?

Here are a few examples of the most valuable types of content for brick-and-mortar business owners:

- **Video**: Create a brief video that highlights your company's unique qualities, showing your prospective and existing customers how things look on "the inside" is a great way to inject that P2P philosophy into the relationship with your customers. Don't be scared to peel back the curtain a little, as it'll separate you from your competitors.
- **Press releases**: Every now and then, a local business does something press-worthy. Highlight your achievements by submitting a press release to local and national media outlets.
- **Blog posts**: If your business is in an advisory role like financial planning, law, fitness training, or psychology, blog posts could bring in online search traffic when people turn to the Internet for answers to simple questions.
- **Facebook fan pages**: Social media is about more than getting people to "like" your page— it's about connecting with your audience. There

are more than one billion Facebook users worldwide, and the average American spends at least a couple hours glued to Facebook each day. It's clearly in your best interest to be there, too. This will also allow you to start ongoing relationships with future customers.

- **Reviews**: A quick word of caution here—don't buy fake reviews. While you should encourage your customers to write reviews (reading positive reviews from other customers is a major selling strategy, especially online), make sure you're also monitoring those reviews so that you can respond to negative comments. You can also have your VA handle this by monitoring the reviews weekly and sending the negative comments to you. Of course, be sure not to let negative comments get you down. It seems that negative people have more time to spare than positive people do!

Now, I'm not saying that you need to get involved with all of these types of tasks. Your virtual team can certainly handle them all, but ultimately, they might not fit your business model or your target industry.

It's great to try a little of everything, and you can use tools such as Facebook's Page Insights and Google Analytics to get clear data on which types of content are creating the most buzz for your business. An SEO VA is the perfect team member to help you evaluate this information.

What Is "Good" Content?

The digital world is already full of content. Unfortunately, most of it is just clutter and pretty distractions.

Let's start by looking at some of the content that keeps you plugged into your private life:

- Every few minutes, your phone vibrates with a text message.
- Right now, your Facebook friends are posting status updates that you'll read later, about thoughts they're having or places they're visiting.
- Your personal e-mail is slowly filling up with "one-time offers" from every retail store that has ever asked for your e-mail address when you made a purchase.

All of that is content—and much of it will get your attention. Now let's consider the content you engage with on a professional level:

- You search through LinkedIn to connect with people you just met at a networking event, clicking through to their profiles and websites to learn more about them.
- Your work e-mail is copied in on an important conversation that someone thought you should be involved in.
- You attend a webinar highlighting critical information that will affect your industry or help you win new business.

- You download a white paper to learn more about a topic that you believe will help your business or position within a company.

Finally, let's consider the type of content you purposefully seek out. Answer these questions to discover what content is actually enriching your life:

- Who do you *really* follow online? These are the people you actively seek out by visiting their blogs, searching their social media posts, and making it a point to watch, listen to, or read the content they release.
- When was the last time you had a personal or professional problem you went online to solve by digesting a piece of content?
- When was the last time you took action on a piece of content that moved your business forward?

Good content might be a free, fifty-page e-book you received for opting in on a website that shows you how to build a blog to grow your business. Or it might be a five-page white paper you download that offers incredible insights on your target market so that you can approach potential customers more successfully. It could be a ten-part video series that teaches you how to create, launch, and promote a podcast, or the infographic you discovered on Pinterest that offers productivity-boosting tips for entrepreneurs who work from home.

All of these examples are considered evergreen content, which means they will transcend time because of their high

THE CASE FOR CONTENT

quality and enduring relevancy. Evergreen content should be able to solve problems and identify new opportunities, while at the same time being able to stand the test of time. As a result, it will be consumed, remembered, and shared regularly.

Just because a blog post shows up on the first page of a Google search doesn't mean it has the answers you need. Likewise, just because your website has a high ranking on Google doesn't mean it will translate into enduring traffic for your site or increased sales.

Too many people think the phrase "content is king" means the website with the most blog posts and videos wins—but that's just not true. It's the online portal with the most high-quality, commented on, and shared content that really wins.

It's easy to produce poor content; for example:

- Content that is simply created for the sake of producing something. Writing or talking about something primarily because you feel obligated to do so rarely leads to good content.
- Content that has no real point—it's just someone rambling while holding a video camera out in front of his or her face.
- Videos with poor sound quality. There's just no excuse for that.
- Anything that has been "spun" through a software program for the sake of search-engine optimization. Black-hat tactics like this are being wiped out by algorithm changes in search engines.
- Outdated material. Please note that this does not include material on your site that is outdated

simply because it was created a long time ago. This refers to material that was created recently by someone who hasn't stayed in touch with his or her industry and is teaching outdated information.

- Hype. I hate hype—it's the drug we use to anesthetize our audiences and ourselves when there's no real meat to deliver.

Too many people have hopped on the content bandwagon without any thought as to where they're headed or if anyone is really following them. After all, isn't the whole point of leadership supposed to be about having some followers?

What makes crappy content even worse is that it costs business owners time and money to produce—and it's a waste of both. Content should not be viewed as something you "do" as if it were on a long checklist of items on your daily agenda. Instead, content should be viewed as something you *get* to do. It's a privilege.

I believe that if your content isn't genuinely solving a problem, entertaining your audience, or motivating the consumer to take positive action, it's not content. It's just clutter. It's this mentality that makes it so important for you to know who you're targeting the content toward. Today, it's probably not who you think it is!

The P2P (People-to-People) Philosophy

I'm an old-school guy who comes from a corporate background. Every job I've ever worked, no matter what position

I held, had a B2B (business-to-business) or B2C (business-to-consumer) focus. But now that I'm a business owner starting, marketing, and building businesses in today's environment, I've shifted my mindset. Now, I prefer to focus on a P2P (people-to-people) philosophy grounded in the awareness that people want to do business with other people.

Despite all the time and money that goes into corporate branding, people don't choose to do business with a company because of a logo design or a mission statement. They choose to do business with a particular brand because of personal experiences with the products or services—and just as importantly, because of the people who represent those products and services.

Your customers want to be your friends. They want to get to know the authority figure behind the business that's taking their money. Most importantly, they want to be treated like real human beings instead of like faceless names on invoices. If a customer tweets at a company with a question, he or she wants to get a reply in real time from a real person. The fact that such an interaction is possible is the beauty of online content platforms today.

James Wedmore is a marketing authority who teaches people how to leverage YouTube to brand themselves and their products or services at his blog JamesWedmore.com. James has experienced the phenomenon of P2P through his YouTube videos.

Once James creates a video, uploads it to YouTube, and promotes it to his mailing list, he moves onto his next project (which is usually another video). Meanwhile, the video he's just uploaded is still sitting there in cyberspace, waiting to interact with anyone who chooses to click on it.

Let's say you watch one of James's videos and you like it. What would you do next? You'd probably watch another. After watching several of these videos, you would probably feel like you knew James if you saw him speaking at a live event because he does such a great job of showcasing his genuine self through his content.

CASE STUDY #9

Joshua Van Den Broek, Principal Exercise Physiologist
Fitco Health Technologies

Joshua Van Den Broek is one of those guys (we've all seen them before) who just can't resist helping others. Don't hold it against him—it's just part of his nature. He created Fitco Health Technologies (Fitco.net.au) straight after completing his university degree in Exercise Physiology so that he could do just that—help others.

I first met Joshua through a members-only business group for which I had previously been a conference speaker. Upon hearing that I was due to undergo invasive spinal fusion surgery in April 2012, Joshua contacted me to give me some advice about what I could do to improve my rate of recovery post surgery.

After my surgery, I got in touch with Joshua to speak with him about how we could fast-track my recovery. Joshua is used to working with his clients in person at his facility, but because of the distance between us, we did a full assessment over Skype and I submitted some photos so he could analyze my posture more closely. He prescribed a tailor-made program with specific exercises for me to perform and checked in with me a few times along the way to keep me on track.

It worked. My recovery was faster than I expected. Since then, Joshua and I have become friends, and he finally got around to telling me about his VAs and how he works with them.

Why Virtual Staffing?

When Joshua first heard about virtual staffing, he was a solopreneur and had experienced both the highs and lows of running a local small business. He decided that he could no longer perform all the roles necessary to allow his business to be profitable and provide the flexibility and freedom that he ultimately desired.

He knew he needed to build a team in order to achieve his vision, but he had a shoestring budget. Hiring a virtual staff was the only logical choice for him, as he could have access to a solid team at a reduced rate.

He started with outsourcing specific one-off tasks such as website development and graphic design for print marketing materials before hiring additional VAs on a more permanent basis for roles that entailed repetitive tasks.

The time Joshua freed up by hiring these virtual team members allowed him to grow his local team and expand the number of his clinics in Sydney, Australia. It also allowed him to focus on additional projects that he was passionate about, such as content creation and marketing for his blog at MyExercisePhysiologist.com.

Without the growth of his virtual team to support his local team, Joshua would not have been able to systemize Fitco Health Technologies to the extent that he has. Today, all aspects of his business are documented and reside as a fluid resource on an intranet, where all team members can access and update them.

Now that Joshua has the time to focus on growing his business rather than just running it day to day, he is considering other possibilities, such as franchising, speaking, and additional online ventures.

Joshua's Hurdles

Joshua had a few issues when he first started out hiring virtual staff, most of them due to his own lack of recruitment skills. With a bit of trial and error, he concluded that finding a candidate that was a good fit for his company came down to two things:

- Communication. He learned that he could accelerate the screening process for interviews by asking candidates to submit a voice recording in his job posting. This not only gave a fair indication of their spoken English skills, but also weeded out the applicants who were not willing to go the extra mile.
- Infectious enthusiasm. Joshua knew that all the skills required for the roles that he was hiring for could be easily learned with good training resources. However, the personality traits of the candidates could not. His most successful hires were those with infectious enthusiasm and willingness to learn.

Another of Joshua's own newbie mistakes proved to be a hurdle for his company. He intially had virtual staff from the Philippines take the bulk of his inbound phone calls using Skype. While the calls were handled adequately by his staff, clients often complained about the quality of the phone line (due to the virtual team members' Internet connection speeds). Joshua experienced a notable drop in sales due to this issue. He overcame this hurdle by moving that particular task to an Australian-based phone service.

Joshua's Best Practices

- **Treat your virtual team just as you would your local team.** Team members who are spread across the globe are no less important than team members who operate from your office.

- **Clearly communicate with your virtual team.** It is important that you articulate task objectives clearly, leaving no room for misinterpretation. This is particularly important since English may be a second language for some of your team members. Before signing off on a task brief, have them repeat back to you their understanding of the task so you can make any clarifications on the spot.

Joshua's Tools of the Trade

Here are the top three tools Joshua utilizes when working with his virtual team:

- **Skype** (Skype.com): Perfect for conducting interviews, holding meetings, and receiving phone calls via Internet connection.
- **Trello** (Trello.com): Joshua uses this project-management tool to create lists, set tasks, store files, track project status, and receive deliverables. Best of all, it's free!
- **Google Sites** (Google.com/sites): Systemize your business by creating your own company intranet where you can store all your systems and training materials for your team. Another freebie!

Joshua's ability to see the true value of his virtual team and respect the role they play in his business has helped him to grow his business locally and has created the opportunity for him to make a global impact by helping others through his online projects. This perfect marriage of old-school business principles and a "new-school" business mindset (working with virtual staff, using blogging and social media to engage with clients, etc.) is something I feel every entrepreneur today has to incorporate sooner or later—or get left behind.

The Importance of Being Remembered

Why are you ultimately thinking about creating content? It's to be remembered. It's to be seen as a leader or a go-to source in your industry—someone who is trustworthy and knowledgeable. You want to be seen as the one person to whom fans, followers, and customers turn when they need answers, support, motivation, or entertainment.

There's no better way to be remembered than as yourself—and if you focus on our P2P philosophy, your personality will clearly shine through in your content. In many ways, the P2P philosophy is the true reason that you're creating content in the first place and working to make it as enduring and ever-green as possible.

The content required to do this *must* include *you*—your personality, your stories, and your expertise. This is the one thing you can't outsource and the one thing you shouldn't want to outsource. People will find you with this content, and you will make an impression on them. Ultimately, this impression will cause a reaction—or, as it's known in the world of business, a transaction!

Even though you're going to be injecting a lot of yourself into your content, you don't have time to research it because you're running a business. You also don't have time to design it, edit it, upload it, publish it, or market it. Fortunately, this is where your virtual team steps in.

Getting Your Virtual Team to Do (Almost) All the Work for You

As we've established, your content ultimately needs to come from you. If it doesn't, it will surely fall flat on its face when it tries to capitalize on the P2P philosophy that is necessary in today's business landscape.

Once the content has been created, you're ready to get to the part you've been waiting for: getting other people to do the rest of the work for you.

I know that when I say "work," it means different things to different people—so when it comes to content creation and marketing, I've broken work down into the following categories:

- **Research**: This category involves researching potential blog posts, videos, podcast episodes, and more. Researchers should also check up on what your company's competitors are doing.

- **Creation**: Everything from basic content creation to info-product (downloadable digital products sold exclusively online) creation.

- **Promotion**: Publish your content and then get it out there for the world to devour!

- **Ongoing marketing**: Once your content goes live, it's time to make sure it is found, consumed, and shared.

We'll now discuss tasks that fall under each of these categories and discover which members of your team will be responsible for handling the work. Even if you don't have all of the VAs mentioned in the action plan below, the plan is still a good framework of how information needs to move. Per-project hires found on Fiverr or Craigslist can quickly fulfill tasks such as designing an e-book cover. It all depends on the level of quality you're looking for and whether or not you're looking to build an ongoing working relationship with someone.

Research

The following research process can be used to create blog posts, videos, podcasts, e-books, infographics, and even some information products. The objective here is to simply gather the raw material you'll need to build on. Keep in mind that nothing about this process is etched in stone. You can tweak to your heart's content to get the best results.

Conducting Research Before Creating Your Product	
Action	**Team Member Responsible**
Make a list of the words, phrases, or people needed to create the content you have in mind. Then, e-mail your GVA to become the main point of contact.	you
Conduct research using the Google Keyword Tool (GoogleKeywordTool.com), Google Trends (Google.com/trends), and YouTube to find the most popular and relevant content.	GVA or SEO VA
Copy and paste links from each platform's five most popular pieces of content into a Google Drive document. This document will be shared with you once it's completed.	GVA or SEO VA
Once you're notified of the shared document, open it and decide what kind of content you want to create.	you

Creation and Publication

Now that you've completed some research, let's see what it looks like to create various types of content from everything you've done so far. Keep in mind that the step-by-step actions described below to create blog posts, marketing videos, e-books, and white papers are a continuation of the research you just did.

Let's take a look at the process you can follow to create a blog post.

Creating a Blog Post	
Action	**Team Member Responsible**
Remember when I said you shouldn't outsource your content creation? I was serious. Sit down and write your blog post using the research that your GVA and SEO team members put together. Then, upload it to Dropbox.	you
Check the blog post for grammar and spelling errors. Make sure it is laid out with subheadings and correct formatting for your approval.	content writer or GVA
Load blog post into WordPress as a draft and embed any necessary images, videos, or screenshots. Complete final formatting and add URL links.	GVA
Publish blog post.	GVA or you

Next you'll find the process you can use to create a marketing video. Please note that you can also replicate this process to create podcast episodes.

Creating a Video	
Action	**Team Member Responsible**
Create a title and video outline based on earlier research and list discussion points in a Google Drive document or by sharing a Word file with your video editor and VPM via Dropbox.	you
Provide feedback and make suggestions, notifying you via e-mail when the document is updated.	video editor and VPM
Shoot the video and send the raw HD file to the video editor.	you
Send you a rough cut of the edit as a low-resolution file. This should include background music, intro and outro bumpers, and any text that you want to show up on the screen.	video editor
Note of any changes you want to be made, indicating the time where the change should appear. For example, you can write, "1:34—add text pop 'Free for this week!'" Send the file to your video editor so that he or she can produce a final cut.	you
Finish the final cut and upload the HD version to Dropbox.	video editor
Transcribe video in full and save it as a separate Word document so that it can be used later in places such as a blog post or YouTube description.	GVA

Publishing an e-book is a great way to build authority and produce something a little more substantial for your online followers to get their teeth into. It's also a perfect opt-in magnet—a piece of content you can use to build an online mailing list.

Creating a White Paper or E-book	
Action	Team Member Responsible
Write a basic outline of the e-book based on the research your GVA has put together. You don't need a title yet, but it's always a good idea to have a working title to guide your vision for the book. Send the outline to the content writer.	you
Create the first draft of the e-book and make notes to suggest where images and/or charts and graphs should go. Then, send the draft to the GVA.	content writer
Find images via royalty-free image websites. Add the images to Dropbox.	GVA
Make final tweaks and share the document with the graphic designer.	content writer
Take the e-book and images from Dropbox and create a cover design and first draft of the complete e-book. Place the file in Dropbox for review.	graphic designer
Review e-book. Give final feedback to the graphic designer.	you and graphic designer
Upload the e-book to your servers. Add an opt-in form if it's a freebie or a "buy now" button if you're selling it as a digital product.	web developer

The transcribe approach to creating an e-book or white paper is a great way to turn your live speaking events, podcasts, long-form videos, or webinars into solid pieces of content that can be used as awesome giveaways for your subscribers and customers. You can also use this approach to create a product to sell on Amazon.

This step-by-step plan doesn't involve the research portion we discussed at the beginning of this section. Finish that before following the plan below.

Creating a Product to Sell on Amazon	
Action	Team Member Responsible
Gather any recordings that you want to use to create the e-book and send them to your GVA to be transcribed. Please note that you can also use a transcription service if your GVA is busy doing other work, as this will tie him or her up for a few days.	you
Collate recordings and transcribe audio in full.	GVA or transcription service
Review the transcription and cut out any material that isn't needed. Make notes in the transcription so the content writer knows which pieces of content correspond with the sections you want produced and finalized.	you
Review the outline and begin turning the transcription into a book. This does not mean simply copying and pasting. Transcribed audio reads much differently than it sounds, so the writer will need to go through and tweak the transcription to make it easier to read. Send you a rough draft to review.	content writer

Action	Team Member Responsible
Review the first draft. Make changes and give feedback before uploading the updated file to Dropbox.	you
Make necessary revisions and do a final edit to ensure grammar and punctuation are correct. Send a final version of the e-book content to the graphic designer.	content writer
Create a cover image and lay out the content in the internal pages. Work with the GVA to compile and insert any necessary images. Send a draft of the finished product to you for final approval.	graphic designer and GVA
Approve e-book.	you
Distribute e-book to Amazon or any other platforms you'll use to sell it or give it away.	GVA and web developer

Promotion

Now that you've created and published your content, it's time to help the world discover it. There's one important piece of advice I'd like to give you: how often you choose to publish content is up to you. Though you have VAs working for you now, don't make the mistake of creating content just because you can. Quality trumps quantity.

For promoting content, I suggest creating a schedule or checklist that your team can follow every time a new piece of content is published. A promotional checklist creates consistency and helps you plan accordingly. Being able to press the autopilot button is beautiful stuff!

Take what you can from the schedule below to create

a time frame for promoting your most recent content. We'll tackle ongoing marketing in a bit, I promise!

This publishing plan can apply to almost any type of content, but I'm going to use a blog post as an example. You're going to see just how valuable your GVA can be.

Creating a Promotion Plan	
Action	Team Member Responsible
Share the content you've created on your personal social media accounts, such as your Facebook fan page, Twitter, and Google+.	GVA
Share content on your LinkedIn profile and with your LinkedIn groups. (Note: It's a good idea to join LinkedIn groups made up of your peers and those for the market you're trying to reach. For example, if your company helps local businesses market themselves online, you should join local marketing groups and groups with the clients you're trying to reach, such as dentists, lawyers, and contractors. This gives your content a larger reach.)	GVA
Schedule tweets to go out every four to six hours for the two days following the content's publication. Instead of just tweeting the link to your article, share a "tweetable" comment from your post instead—something that stands out. These "tweetables" are typically shared more often than simple article headlines.	GVA
Have the content bookmarked on sites such as StumbleUpon, Digg, and Reddit.	GVA or SEO VA

Action	Team Member Responsible
Look through your post and identify anyone you may have mentioned or linked to. Contact these people directly with an e-mail (already prewritten using a template) to notify them that you've mentioned them positively in a piece of content in case they would like to share it.	GVA
Write an e-mail notifying your mailing list about the piece of content you've just published.	you (for a more personal touch)
Share the featured image from your post on sites such as Pinterest and Flickr.	GVA

Ongoing Marketing

This is a slightly more tactical, long-term approach to building up your company's brand online by optimizing the content you've created.

Optimizing Your Content	
Action	**Team Member Responsible**
Podcasts and videos: Have podcasts and videos transcribed and placed in a "blog bank" that can be used for future posts on your own website and for guest posts for others. This content can also be summarized and shared on social bookmarking sites like Tumblr, StumbleUpon, Reddit, and Digg.	GVA

table continued on following page...

… *continued from previous page*

Optimizing Your Content	
Action	**Team Member Responsible**
Blog posts: Create internal links from your new content to older content that's relevant. This will help boost natural SEO scores while also giving visitors the chance to discover some of your older evergreen content.	SEO VA or GVA
Blog comments: Respond to comments on your blog posts, Facebook page, or YouTube channel. This is necessary if you want to build a stronger connection with your audience, particularly on your blog. Remember the P2P philosophy? This is something I wouldn't suggest outsourcing.	you
Infographics: Produce a cool infographic based on one of your videos or blog posts. This is way easier to do than most people think. Have your GVA share it on an active infographic-distribution site.	graphic designer and/or GVA
Slide document sharing: Convert your transcriptions into a PowerPoint or Keynote presentation and share them on websites such as Docstoc and SlideShare for additional exposure.	graphic designer or GVA

FREEDOM SPOTLIGHT

Natalie Sisson
Digital Nomad
The Suitcase Entrepreneur

With an online brand name like the Suitcase Entrepreneur, you might expect Natalie Sisson to be homeless—and in a way, she is! Natalie's location independence has been the key to her phenomenal success as more and more solopreneurs are aspiring to live their lives on their own terms, just like her. When she started SuitcaseEntrepreneur.com almost four years ago, Natalie wanted to make sure it wouldn't tie her down in one place. She knew that she could manage everything from her computer because all of the central ingredients of her content marketing business—namely, blogging, podcasts, and videos—could be handled with a simple Internet connection.

❯ The Problem

Early on in the development of her company, even though she was extremely dedicated, Natalie realized she had no clue how to run some of the necessary areas of her business, like accounting and customer support. Still, she continued to struggle along on her own; her determined, competitive nature didn't take kindly to any sort of loss of control in her business. (Sounds a little like superhero syndrome, doesn't it?) Ultimately she reached out for help on the eve of a two-month trip to Africa, where Internet connections would be scarce.

❯ The Solution

Natalie went about building a dedicated team of VAs who all live in completely different countries. She has a GVA in India, a podcast editor in the Philippines, a video editor in the Netherlands, a project manager and systems analyst in Belgium, a web and tech guru in the United States, a graphic designer in the United Kingdom, and her "Chief Happiness Officer"—who handles all her customer support—also based in the United States. With her team members spread so widely across the globe, she tends to work with each of them one on one instead of bringing them all together on a regular basis. However, they do all interact together via a project-management system.

> The Outcome

The most important lesson Natalie has learned from working with VAs is how to work on her business rather than in it. By hiring reliable VAs, Natalie has had the opportunity to step back from micromanaging and tedious technical work to instead focus on ways to truly grow her business. When she is off traveling and doing the things she loves, she feels confident that her employees will manage the business smoothly—as if they were clones of Natalie herself!

At a first glance, you might think that content marketing isn't for you. If you think it sounds like an awful lot of work, you're right. You can't just magic up some amazing content out of the blue. Content marketing takes some planning and strategy. But before you discount it completely, remember why we looked at content as a viable way to build your brand, your customer reach, and your business in the first place.

Social media expert Amy Porterfield, who blogs at AmyPorterfield.com, is regarded as one of the most influential people in the world of Facebook marketing. She has helped thousands of small business owners navigate the difficult world of advertising on the most popular social media channel in the world. But she is also a prolific content marketer—researching, creating, and publishing some of the best blog and podcast content online in her niche. She does this all to build her brand and to educate, and she does it very well.

Content marketing is about solving problems and getting answers to questions that your customers have. It's also about entertaining and inspiring your audience and prospective customers to take action based on something that you've presented to them. Taking action is addictive. Once customers act on advice that you've given them, you've got 'em forever—as long as you are true to your word and continue to help them take action.

Typically, the strategy and the planning take more time than the actual creation of the content. Luckily for you, you've got your hardworking team of virtual assistants to help handle the heavy lifting.

SECTION SEVEN

Time to Get Started

As you start to strategize and put processes in place to achieve your own freedom, remember to focus on the core fundamentals of the *Virtual Freedom* mindset, namely

- Your virtual workers are people, not a program.
- Put quality in, get quality out.
- Hire for the role, not the task.
- Super-VAs don't exist.

That last one is the maxim I urge you to appreciate more than anything else. Not a day goes by that I don't receive an e-mail from a busy and stressed-out yet full-of-great-ideas business owner who believes that the answer to all of his or her marketing, customer service, and business administrative problems is a single VA.

As you begin hiring and working with VAs, be smart, follow your gut, and take baby steps. If you've already spent some time and money outsourcing tasks to virtual staff members, you'll know that Rome wasn't built in a day or by just one person.

Your First Six Months

With this in mind, I'm putting a challenge your way: a six-month timeline you can follow to get started. All you need to do is work toward each milestone, just like I did in 2010, and with a little hard work (and a bit of luck with your hiring!), you should be well on your way.

Month #1

Hire a general VA and spend some time training him or her on a number of different tasks from the first list of your 3 Lists to Freedom—the things you don't like doing.

These no doubt directly relate to the day-to-day running of your business and take up a lot of your time, so start eliminating them immediately.

Month #2

Focus on your second list from the 3 Lists to Freedom: things you don't know how to do. Are there tasks that your GVA can handle for you?

If so, pass them along. If not, ask your GVA to start researching freelance VAs that can handle these tasks for you, even on a per-project basis. Just get them off your plate!

Month #3

This month is all about the third list: things you shouldn't be doing. Remember I said that this one requires a lot of thought. So spend some time doing just that—thinking.

Once you've assigned a few of these tasks to your GVA

(or to freelancers, if the GVA can't do them), it's time to begin planning your next hire.

Month #4

By now you're probably starting to breathe a little easier. You are hopefully recovering from superhero syndrome, and you're starting to see the benefits of having your GVA (and other virtual workers you may have hired on a per-project or part-time basis) handling a number of tasks for you.

It's time to make your next hire. In today's world I suggest this be an SEO/Internet marketing VA—someone who can help your GVA to market your business more thoroughly and effectively online.

Month #5

Your SEO/Internet marketing VA should be working in tandem with your GVA now, and although you've probably not yet seen a huge increase in website traffic (it takes a few months of solid SEO work for that to start taking shape), if you've hired well, you're definitely seeing some serious action on your social media channels and your blogging and other content marketing is starting to really take off.

Keep working hard on the content side of things this month, as your VAs will need new, original content to help market and promote your business.

Perhaps you can start thinking about taking a couple of weeks off at this point. Seriously. Show your GVA that you trust them, and turn over the day-to-day work related to managing your SEO/Internet marketing VA, and let's see how they do together without you.

Month #6

If you took that break (I hope you did), you've discovered how things went between your VAs without your involvement. How did it work out?

If you didn't take the time off, that's okay—I understand. I've been there. However, put it on the schedule soon! You're now officially half a year into your virtual freedom mission. How is it going? Please feel free to e-mail me directly at Chris@ChrisDucker.com to let me know.

At this point I want you to go back to your 3 Lists to Freedom (see how important those little lists have become?), and cross off all the things that you're no longer handling yourself. Whatever is left is your "eliminate list" for the next six months.

You've come a long way, and I'm proud of you. As you continue to grow your team, develop your strategies, and put your processes in place, remember to think long term and think about roles, not tasks.

Most importantly, think virtual.

Chances are good that your competitors already have, but the good news is you have, too, and you might just be ahead of the curve in developing your own virtual team of superstars!

Conclusion

Now that we're (almost) at the end of the book, I hope that I've achieved what I set out to do—to show you how building a team of virtual employees can give you the freedom to work *on* your business instead of being trapped working *in* it.

In 2010, when I decided to stop being a stressed-out, micromanaging business owner so that I could achieve my goal of becoming a virtual CEO, I never could have truly appreciated what having that virtual freedom would mean for myself, my family, and my business. Now I have the time to help my kids with their homework, I take regular vacations, I've removed Friday from my work week, and I get to focus on big-picture thinking about my business to move it forward more regularly—all while my virtual (and some physical) employees keep things running day to day.

That life-changing year has allowed me to invest in my work with a whole new focus—one that is freedom-based with an abundant mindset that truly allows me to make the most of my life as an entrepreneur. Developing the ability to fight off superhero syndrome and live a life based on my own terms has been rewarding to say the least.

I wish you all the best on your own journey towards *virtual freedom*!

Top 10 Virtual Team-Building Mistakes (and How to Avoid Them!)

Let's get one thing straight—you're going to make mistakes. Developing processes that work for your unique organization and personality will take some trial and error—there are no magic pills to pop, and nothing works out of the gate. But that's okay—mistakes are the best way to learn.

However, some mistakes are repeat offenders and can be made by both newbies and seasoned entrepreneurs.

From the thousands of e-mails I've received over the years from entrepreneurs struggling with outsourcing, I've compiled the following list of the ten most repeated mistakes. These are mistakes that can and should be avoided.

1. Mismanagement or a Lack of Willingness to Manage Your Team

Out of sight, out of mind—right? Not quite. Though you don't see your virtual staff on a daily basis, they still have to be supervised. In fact, in the first few months, they'll have to be managed a lot. Employee mismanagement is a mistake often made because an entrepreneur doesn't anticipate the amount of time he or she will have to devote to keeping track of employees. After all, isn't that why you're outsourcing—to free up more time?

Absolutely—but you still need to do some intial legwork. As with any new employee in a brick-and-mortar company, an outsourcer has to be trained. Whether the position is part-time or full-time, you have to integrate each person into your company and teach him or her your way of doing things.

The three principal errors business owners make in managing virtual employees are

- **Not managing at all**: This happens a lot with entrepreneurs who have no background in outsourcing. They think, "I'm hiring an expert. He or she should know what to do." While that may be true, you still need to set milestones, review work, and make sure the VA isn't experiencing any problems.

  Call it syncing with your employees. It doesn't even have to happen every day, but it does need to be done. In a physical office, supervisors normally check up on each employee's progress during a weekly meeting. When it comes to outsourcing, you may have to do it twice or even three times a week in the beginning. Checking in doesn't have to take a lot of time. It could be a five-minute chat every morning or night so that you can ask about your VA's schedule for the day or request a quick progress update.

It's also a good idea to let your virtual workers know about your availability. Tell them you are more than willing to take calls when they have problems or questions. If you don't want to be bothered during certain parts of the day, give them a daily schedule or ask them to leave voicemails.

Be mindful of setting daily schedules if you and the outsourcer live in very different time zones. You don't want to be woken up in the middle of the night—and neither does your VA, which could happen if time zone confusion sets in.

- **Micromanaging**: On the opposite side of the spectrum, we have managers who are paranoid about checking up on everything. This is typical for those who have been burned with outsourcing before and have gone off the deep end. They absolutely must know about everything.

 By everything I mean detailed daily reports, hourly updates, crazy timesheets, phone calls every few minutes, and key loggers or screenshot software on the VA's personal computer so that the micromanaging boss can snoop and spy.

 It's one thing to make sure your team members are doing their work, but it's a whole different ballgame to request so much information that you prevent them from getting anything done. Detailed reports and timesheets take time. If it takes more than thirty minutes each day to fill these out, you're making your team inefficient. Don't call your VA every ten minutes to ask if he or she is done yet.

Focus on your team's finished work unless you've given them jobs that must be handled on an hourly basis, such as answering the phone or providing online customer support.

Limit the time you spend checking up on your employees. A short phone call once a day or a long meeting once or twice a week is often enough to catch up. Anything beyond that takes time and costs you money. Most outsourcers, especially freelance workers, bill for the time it takes to draw up these long reports—and you'll spend hours trying to review them all.

Key loggers and screenshot software only serve to scare your employees or give them the impression that you don't trust them. Unfortunately, if you're going to this extreme, you probably don't trust your workers—and trust is a big part of success in outsourcing. This kind of mistrust is a great way to ensure that your fears will come to light: you won't have a good VA because you'll drive him or her away!

It's hard to work when someone is looking over your shoulder. Honestly, I don't understand people who hire VAs and then spend all their time snooping and checking up on them. It totally defeats the premise behind outsourcing.

- **Not knowing how to manage**: You've probably heard the saying, "Managers can be good employees, but not all employees can be good managers." You can be very good at your job, but that doesn't mean you'll automatically be a good manager. Believe it or not, the vast majority of business owners whom I've come into contact with say that they started out as pretty terrible managers—myself included.

  Most entrepreneurs were employees themselves with zero experience in supervision, or freelancers who suddenly felt the need to expand when they started getting more work. If this is your first time being the boss, expect to make some mistakes—because you'll be making a lot of them. Learn to forgive yourself for your mistakes and turn them into opportunities to learn. This level of self-awareness will strengthen your managerial skills over time. Being a good manager doesn't happen overnight.

  Keep in mind that each person you manage is different—and that he or she is different from you. Do not expect your VA to act the same way you do.

  Finally, remember that being a manager or a supervisor is a job. It takes time, a lot of work, and sometimes more education to get better. If you find yourself needing help, ask for it. Leave your ego at the door—remember what I said about self-awareness?—and ask for help from other business owners in similar positions.

2. Choosing the Wrong Location

When it comes to outsourcing, a lot of your success depends on location, location, location. A mistake in location can often lead to a lot of lost time and money. In the Philippines, for example, traditional business tasks such as transcription work or data entry can be sent to outsourcers in provinces or smaller cities. Labor is cheaper in these places, but the people often do not have a lot of experience, so you can expect some errors. Nontraditional BPO (business-process outsourcing) or KPO (knowledge-process outsourcing) work should be sent to places with better facilities and more experienced and knowledgeable workers. These are usually major cities and their surrounding metropolitan areas, such as—in the case of the Philippines—Manila, Davao, or Cebu.

3. Failing to Analyze Your Virtual Staffing Needs

Once entrepreneurs realize how much time and money they can save by delegating work to virtual staff, they sometimes get outsource-happy and begin outsourcing everything and anything that lands on their desks. Others may want to outsource but become paralyzed before they begin—they don't know what or how to outsource, and they cannot bear to delegate any work.

Before you outsource a task or project, analyze whether

or not it is something that could be handled best by your local staff, yourself, or a virtual worker. Not everything is suitable to assign to a virtual employee—a perfect example is anything related to the written word. Though your local staff is paid more, will they be able to produce a higher-quality document with fewer grammatical errors than an overseas worker? If so, it might be worthwhile to have your local team handle it so that you don't have to spend so much time or money correcting the work.

Many entrepreneurs outsource tasks simply because they don't want to do them—even when the tasks are something they can or should only do themselves. Doing this can unnecessarily double the size of your staff, costing you money, not to mention it being detrimental to your business, if you end up outsourcing the wrong tasks or roles.

If something does need to be outsourced, it's important to break the project down into manageable tasks so that you can track it easily and figure out if you need to send it to one VA or to a team.

Go back to your 3 Lists to Freedom here and use them as a guide to see exactly what you needed or wanted to outsource in the first place. This will help you figure out what type of worker should handle the task for you.

4. Following the Wrong Outsourcing Model

It's easy to find get-rich-quick formulas that promote one-size-fits-all programs for outsourcing. But not all businesses are the same. They are different sizes and have different markets, different budgets, and wildly different needs. If you want to find an assistant to do affiliate marketing, you obviously won't buy a book detailing how some Fortune 100 company succeeded in outsourcing management-level work. Likewise, if you're an architectural firm, it won't do you any good to buy a program that only tells you how to hire a VA to set up WordPress sites. Your outsourcing model needs to fit you like a glove. Finding the right fit takes a lot of work—and many people give up when faced with hard work.

Another problem with some of the outsourcing advice out there is that some of it paints an incomplete picture of how to outsource, stopping after describing the hiring process or only showing you how to train your new team.

Outsourcing is a very powerful tool, but you need to know how to use it. To do this, you need to step back and learn more about your business, the type of outsourcing model that best suits you and your business, as well as the initial setup of the outsourcing process (as I've outlined in Sections 1 to 3).

To find the right outsourcing model, you need to get down into the trenches. Talk to other people who are already using virtual workers. You can do this by searching for groups on social networking sites such as Facebook and LinkedIn that focus on outsourcing and working with virtual staff. Ask how they're implementing their virtual teams. Get educated, and most of all, be willing to put in the work.

5. Inadequate Compensation (Also Known as Being a Tight-Ass!)

Lately, the term "outsourcing" seems to be synonymous with the word "cheap"—as in, cheap labor, cheap overhead costs, cheap benefits, and ultimately, cheap products. This is something I'm hoping to change. Outsourcing certainly isn't cheap, but it is cost-effective—and that includes salaries for your virtual assistants. Besides, people who are called cheap are seldom happy, and neither are their workers—and an unhappy worker will always do a poor job.

Compensation that both you and your employee feel is fair can be a hard balance to strike. People rarely think they're getting paid fairly—otherwise those bigwigs from mega-corporations wouldn't expect $1,000,000 bonuses on top of their bazillion-dollar salaries. My definition of fair compensation is something higher than market price but lower than what you would pay the outsourcer's counterpart at home.

When you consider that some offshore VAs routinely get paid 150 percent less than their onshore counterparts, it becomes clear that you'll have to depend on the experience level of the VA, to determine how low you can go. Many Internet marketing "guru" types love to sell the idea of paying a VA $250 a month to handle all the drudge work. While that idea might seem tempting, it isn't always the case, and most of the time they say these things to get you excited about the concept of outsourcing so that you end up buying their revolutionary online product. Be realistic—what type of quality is someone going to bring to your business if you're paying them $1.56 per hour?

As I've mentioned countless times in interviews and at speaking engagements, adequate compensation is determined by the virtual worker's experience, location, and market prices—and as demand for virtual staffing increases, salaries are changing quite a bit.

*For up-to-date information on Filipino salaries, you can head to the regularly updated guide to paying Filipino VAs on my blog at **ChrisDucker.com/VAPay***

If you are hiring outsourcers who have no experience, you should use the local markets that they are based in to determine their rates. However, if you're hiring experienced outsourcers who have done online and offline work, you'll need to be ready to pay them based on their experience level, their expectations for the job, and where their experience falls in the range of acceptable salaries for their positions.

One of the simplest ways to build a team you can trust is to pay your VAs fair prices that take into account what they want to receive, market norms, and what you're comfortable paying. Make an attractive offer that is considerate and reasonable to you and your staff.

If you can only afford so much, find another perk to offer, such as the opportunity to advance, paid vacation time, free products, commission bonuses, or scheduled raises. If you're a coach or offer another relevant service, you could even offer employees some of your time in exchange for their work.

6. Inability to Recognize the Outsourced Site's Culture

After picking the right location, it is absolutely critical that you get to know the people who work there. While a VA is expected to adapt to his or her employer's culture, there are always a few things you cannot change. This includes work ethic, time constraints, the VA's social status, certain language quirks, and his or her overall attitude. Ask your staff for a few tourism websites that showcase the culture side of their country, if you're working with people outside of your own domain. It'll help you get on the same page as them.

For example, Southeast Asians tend to be rather shy and very polite. Their language includes designations for big brother, boss, and professional. They have a clear social structure that teaches them to respect their elders. If you put people with these qualities on the collections department of a credit card company where they'll have to address everyone by first name and be rude to late-paying customers, it's going to take them a while adapt. I'm not saying it's impossible because it's being done—but it will take some training. Likewise, if your VA comes from a background where people do not speak unless spoken to, you might take his or her silence in meetings as a lack of initiative or imagination.

Adapting to a culture goes both ways, and you need to give as much importance to your virtual worker's culture as he or she is expected to give to yours. Respect your differences. That may seem like common sense, but it's a problem that routinely frustrates entrepreneurs. They expect offshore freelancers to act like them, and they alienate their team members instead of accepting each worker's differences.

The key to building a cohesive remote team is to recognize your employee's differences and to embrace them.

7. Lack of Proper Structure and Communication

If you have a manager who doesn't want to manage, a team of people who all work different hours with no knowledge of what the others are doing, and no system for communication, you're setting yourself up for an outsourcing failure. Virtual teams need a lot of stability and structure. They need set protocols and contingency plans to back them up. This is one of the main reasons that I suggest having a GVA or project manager create a regularly updated operations manual. If someone leaves, you'll have a rundown of what the worker did on a daily basis along with any processes that he or she followed.

Some entrepreneurs find this to be too rigid and think it chokes creativity. On the contrary, structure can boost creativity. For example, having set brainstorming or watering hole hours lets your staff know that ideas are encouraged and even expected and prompts a steady flow of innovation.

Communicating is the hardest part of virtual working. You need to invest in a collaborative platform (such as one of the project-management systems we discussed earlier like Basecamp or Asana) that works for you and your team. If you find one that works well but costs money, do not cut corners—buy it. Also expect that anything that takes one hour to work on face-to-face will likely take twice as long when working with people on the phone. It could take even more time if you're talking to four people on a conference call.

Good communication involves more than having the right technology or structure. If your VAs are overseas, culture plays a part, too. They might have their own ways of saying things or certain taboos, so I suggest doing some Internet research to get up to speed with what their culture is all about.

You and your team need to do some groundwork to find that groove. Once you do, the distance won't make a difference.

8. Reluctance to Adapt to a Virtual Work Environment

When you work with remote workers, you'll start to rely heavily on technology and become dependent on the fast pace of the Internet. For traditionalists who are set in their ways, it's easy to get left behind. You'll need to invest a certain amount in training for your team and perhaps in new software. While it's no longer unusual to hire a VA who is in his or her forties or an Internet marketer in his or her twenties, some entrepreneurs still find it difficult to accept this fact.

A fifty-year old dry-cleaning business owner may be unreceptive to the ideas that a twenty-three-year-old SEO specialist has to offer, based solely on the SEO VA's age. Likewise, a twenty-four-year-old Internet marketer might be dismissive of a thirty-seven-year-old VA's advice on managing online files—even if the older worker does have fifteen years of offline and online experience as an executive assistant.

Prejudices like these will only hold you back. The only thing constant on the Internet is change, and that happens quickly. You either have to keep up or get washed out. This is the new way of doing business—or, as I sometimes call it, the virtual business lifestyle.

9. Underutilizing Virtual Talent

While a lot of entrepreneurs work hard to make sure their online businesses are sustainable in the long term, they don't always think about their staff members in the same way. Some entrepreneurs view their VAs as temps or as a cheap way to staff the company during its startup phase. Once the business gets bigger, the entrepreneur intends to rent an office and grow the company by employing a full-time office-based staff. For this reason, he or she doesn't give much care to training or managing VAs.

Other entrepreneurs allow their businesses to become top-heavy. They keep promoting themselves and hiring from outside to fill the management ranks despite the fact that their entry-level workers have the qualifications to advance. They simply forget that they can promote their virtual workers, too.

Then there are the business owners who overlook their VAs' abilities entirely because they have a fundamental bias against anyone with a developing-world education, thinking they couldn't possibly match someone with a Western diploma. As misguided as this prejudice is, it's not at all uncommon.

You should never pick your staff based solely on what they can do now. Instead, imagine what they can contribute to your company's growth in the future. Underutilizing virtual talent is a common and costly mistake. An outsourcer, like any employee, can get bored and leave in search of more challenging work.

When you don't recognize your VA's skills at all, he or she will feel undervalued and detached from the company. If you do not think of your team members as important parts of your company, they won't think your company is important either. This often results in poor employee performance or the employee leaving altogether.

Remember, the battle to staff and grow a productive team is won by preventing attrition and learning how to retain and manage your outsourcers. Recruitment and training take time and a lot of money. Instead of looking at your virtual employees in the short term, extend your vision by including them in your company's growth. Nurture each worker's potential and involve him or her as much as you can.

10. Attempting to Outsource Your Understanding

When we say you can outsource everything, that doesn't mean that an outsourcer can take the place of your expertise or knowledge in running your businesses. There are many fly-by-night entrepreneurs out there who read books, pick niches, and decide to become overnight experts on topics they have zero experience in and aren't qualified to talk about. Although they might make a little money, it's easy to see that these types of people don't last very long in the business world.

Likewise, some entrepreneurs outsource parts of their business that they don't understand at all and rely 100 percent on the knowledge of their virtual teams. You may not need to know how to do everything in your business, but you do need to know why it's important or at least have an understanding of how it's done. For example, while you may not necessarily need to know how to build a website using WordPress, you do need to understand why you should build a site using this platform instead of using Drupal or Joomla.

In order for you to effectively run your growing virtual company, you need to learn its nuts and bolts. You cannot fake your way into becoming an expert. You may be able to hire a team of virtual assistants to position you as an expert in your niche or a programmer to build you a site that makes you look legitimate, but you still need to manage your company. You cannot do that unless you know exactly what it is you are doing.

If you want to explore a certain industry, then take the time to learn about it—and then you can hire someone to help position you in the niche. Your credibility will not lie on your staff. It lies solely on you. If you don't know anything about a particular aspect of your business, you can have your team members explain it to you. Ask them why it is needed or why it is important. A really good virtual assistant will be able to give you a step-by-step explanation of why implementing a program or a design is crucial to your business. He or she should also explain how the new program or design will impact your potential growth.

• • •

To wrap up, let's recap a couple of key points. First and foremost, every company is unique. Because of this, it's important to spend time figuring out what you should and should not be outsourcing in the first place. Once you've done that, it pays to figure out to whom you should be outsourcing the work. Is this a job for a domestically based employee or freelancer, or is it something you can pass onto your overseas VA?

The aim of outsourcing isn't to simply offload work. It's about building an efficient, lean business that's managed with a smart attitude and a clear focus toward gaining you—the owner—as much freedom as possible to run and grow your company.

Resources

The following is a complete rundown of all the important websites, services, software, and solutions that are listed in the book, plus a few extra that I've decided to throw in for good measure.

Please be sure to hop over to my blog and get on my subscribers list. Not only will it keep you up to date with all the content that I publish, my speaking schedule, additional projects, and mastermind events, but it'll also get you access to plenty of free resources.

*Go to **ChrisDucker.com** and get started, for free, today!*

Below, I've broken the resources up into different categories and added a one-sentence explanation for each.

Finding and Hiring Virtual Staff

- **Craigslist.org**
  Job posting, freelancing, and more.
- **eaHELP.com**
  US-based virtual-assistant services.
- **Elance.com**
  Job-posting marketplace for freelancing virtual assistants.
- **Freelancer.com**
  Large job-posting marketplace with many international freelancers.

- **HireMyMom.com**
  US-based admin support and services.

- **oDesk.com**
  Job-posting marketplace for freelancing virtual assistants.

- **VirtualStaffFinder.com**
  GVA-matchmaking service (author-owned!).

- **Zirtual.com**
  US-based virtual concierge service.

Training Tools and Resources

- **Lynda.com**
  Business, software, and creative skills training courses.

- **MindTools.com**
  Personal and professional upgrade training and resources.

- **Techsmith.com/Camtasia**
  Screen-recording software for PC; used for training VAs.

- **Techsmith.com/Jing**
  Free 5-min clip screencast recording software for Mac and PC.

- **Techsmith.com/Snagit**
  Screen-capture software (PC and Mac) for training VAs.

- **Telestream.net/ScreenFlow**
  Screen-recording software for Mac users. Great for training VAs.

- **Udemy.com**
  Collection of online courses on limitless topics.

- **VirtualStaffTrainingAcademy.com**
  My VA training course (so you don't have to do it!).

Project-Management Solutions/Software

All of the following software systems allow you to manage and work with your virtual staff within their web-based portal. Some are more robust than others, but basically they all have the same objective—help you and your team stay super-focused and productive.

- **Asana.com**
- **Basecamp.com**
- **HiveDesk.com**
- **Huddle.com**
- **Mindjet.com**
- **TeamworkPM.net**
- **Zendesk.com**

Communication Tools

- **Google.com/hangouts**
  Group video-call software. Perfect for virtual meetings.

- **Google.com/sites**
  Create an online intranet for your company.

- **GoToMeeting.com**
  Video-conferencing software for virtual meetings.

- **GroupMe.com**
  Handy team-messaging tool that also has a great mobile app.

- **MeetingBurner.com**
  Great, easy-to-use software with recording capabilities.

- **Skype.com**
  The number-one video and audio communication tool for working with virtual teams.

Document Sharing and Syncing

- **Dropbox.com**
  File-sharing software that syncs across multiple devices and users.

  Google.com/drive
  Formerly Google Docs; file-sharing for multiple users.

- **Screencast.com**
  Online file storage and sharing, including videos and more.

Productivity Tools and Software

- **Evernote.com**
  Idea collector, sorter, and organizer.
- **LastPass.com**
  Password management tool.
- **RhinoSupport.com**
  Excellent e-mail management and help desk support service.
- **ScheduleOnce.com**
  Scheduling portal to help manage your calendar.
- **Simplenote.com**
  Great mobile app for taking notes on multiple devices.
- **TeuxDeux.com**
  Easy-to-use to-do list manager.
- **TimeandDate.com/holidays**
  List of holidays in differences countries.
- **Trello.com**
  An idea collector and a mini project-management system in one.

One-Off Outsourcing Solutions

- **99designs.com**
  Online marketplace for graphic designers and their customers.
- **Babelverse.com**
  Voice-translation services.
- **Fiverr.com**
  Quick, cheap outsourcing of one-off tasks.
- **Microtask.com**
  Document processing, data entry, and data verification.

Payment Processors and Information

- **ChrisDucker.com/VAPay**
  Additional info and resources for paying your virtual assistants, including PayPal alternatives (constantly being updated!).

- **PayPal.com**
  Online payment processor; perfect for paying virtual staff.

Online Marketing Tools

- **AdRoll.com**
  Smart retargeting that gets your ads seen in the right places.
- **Aweber.com**
  E-mail list–building and marketing software tool.
- **BreakthroughBlogging.com**
  Excellent blogging tutorials and much more.
- **Digg.com**
  Social bookmarking platform.
- **Docstoc.com**
  Sharing platform for online documents and presentations (PowerPoint, Keynote).
- **Fizzle.co**
  Online business-building tutorials and so much more.
- **Google.com/adwords**
  Advertising that promotes your website.
- **Google.com/trends**
  Find out which keywords are trending on Google.
- **GoogleKeywordTool.com**
  Search and collate industry keywords and terms.
- **LeadPages.net**
  Simple way to create landing pages to grow your mailing list.
- **LongTailPro.com**
  Keyword research, tracking, and management tool.
- **MarketSamurai.com**
  Keyword research, tracking, and management tool.
- **PlagiarismChecker.com**
  Check written content for duplicated content online.
- **Reddit.com**
  Social bookmarking website.

- **Shopify.com**
  E-commerce tool that allows you to set up an online store for your products.
- **SlideShare.net**
  Sharing platform for online presentations (PowerPoint, Keynote).
- **StumbleUpon.com**
  Social bookmarking website.

Social Media and Team-Building Tools

- **Facebook.com/about/groups**
  Create a private group for virtual team building.
- **Google.com/plus**
  Google's very own social media platform. Growing rapidly.
- **Instagram.com**
  Image- and video-sharing platform for mobile devices.
- **LinkedIn.com/directory/groups**
  Collection of business groups. Why not start your own?
- **Ning.com**
  Social media platform creator. Build your own Facebook!
- **Pinterest.com**
  Image-based social media platform.
- **Twitter.com**
  Micro-blogging site (follow me: @chrisducker).
- **Yammer.com**
  Corporate social media platform (Facebook for companies).

Podcasting and Video Marketing

- **Animoto.com**
  Easy-to-use online video-editing software.
- **Apple.com/garageband**
  Podcast and audio-file creation for training VAs.
- **Audacity.sourceforge.net**
  Audio recording/editing software. Used in podcasting and training.

- **BuddyPress.org**
  WordPress plugin for publishing podcasts easily.
- **Splasheo.com**
  Customized intro and outro animated clips for online videos.
- **YouTube.com**
  Online video-sharing platform.

Images, Graphics, and Web Development Tools

- **IconArchive.com**
  Huge collection of web icons and additional graphics.
- **IconBeast.com**
  Great collection of web icons and graphics.
- **iStockPhoto.com**
  Great collection of photos, illustrations, and more.

Mobile App Development and Tools

- **iBuildApp.com**
  Platform that allows you to create iPhone and iPad apps.
- **MobileDevHQ.com**
  Mobile app marketing and promotion.
- **ShoutEm.com**
  Easy-to-use mobile-app-creation software.

Additional Resources and Miscellaneous Links

- **Bluehost.com**
  Excellent website hosting and domain name providers.
- **FreshBooks.com**
  Small-business accounting software.
- **WordPress.com**
  The number-one blogging and website-building software out there.
- **WPCurve.com**
  Simple, month-to-month Wordpress tweaks and updates service.

- **Xero.com**
  Online accounting software.

Suggested Reading

All of these online entrepreneurial and small-business marketing resources were mentioned in the book. I suggest digging into all of their archives.

- **AmyPorterfield.com**
  Facebook marketing and advertising advice.
- **BecomeABlogger.com**
  Leslie Samuel's how-to-change-the-world-by-blogging business.
- **BlogMarketingAcademy.com**
  David Risley's blogging-for-business platform.
- **EntrepreneurOnFire.com**
  John Lee Dumas's daily business podcast.
  EventualMillionaire.com
  Jaime Tardy's super-inspiring podcast and blog.
- **JamesWedmore.com**
  Online video and productivity tips.
- **LewisHowes.com**
  Entrepreneurship and lifestyle design help and inspiration.
- **MichaelHyatt.com**
  Leadership, publishing, and personal branding advice.
  SmallBizTrends.com
  Huge small-business knowledge base by Anita Campbell and her team.
- **SuitcaseEntrepreneur.com**
  Natalie Sisson's blog and book.
- **RyanLee.com**
  Online marketing and product creation tips and tactics.
- **SuperFastBusiness.com**
  Online business strategies from James Schramko.
- **TheRiseToTheTop.com**
  Mediapreneurship and more, from David Siteman Garland.

RESOURCES

- **ThinkTraffic.net**
  Corbett Barr's online marketing and traffic generation blog.

Lastly, don't forget to spend some time on the companion website for this book. You'll find all the templates, links to resources, additional content, interviews with successful entrepreneurs that have injected virtual staff into their business, and much, much more.

As a reader of the book you have instant access to everything at **VirtualFreedomBook.com/Reader**—*all for free.*

Gratitude

As with most big projects, there are many people that play a part in getting to a final version. This book was no exception. Thank you to everyone who helped make *Virtual Freedom* a reality.

I would, however, like to extend particular thanks to some of my key supporters on this project:

My wife, Ercille, for putting up with my bouts of rambling in the middle of the night, as one idea after another hit me in bed. Her support was unwavering. Always.

My agent, Kristina Holmes, for helping me finally become a traditionally published author, a goal of mine for as long as I can remember.

Fellow podcaster Srinivas Rao for introducing me to Kristina, paving the way for making this whole thing happen.

My publisher, BenBella Books, for being amazingly easy to work with and providing nonstop help and support throughout the entire process.

Matt Gartland (and team!) for doing the initial edit of the book, helping to make sense of my Britishisms, and carving out a great overall flow for the book.

All the amazing business owners that were part of my

Case Study and Freedom Spotlight sections of the book, for sharing their awesome stories.

Close friend and fellow online entrepreneur Pat Flynn for his steadfast support, countless chitchats via Skype, and simply being there (instead of just "everywhere!").

Fellow freedom-fighting entrepreneur Natalie Sisson for some brilliant book brainstorming sessions and her infectious smile.

My amazing team at Virtual Staff Finder for being awesome teammates, for putting up with my silly jokes, and for making me smile every day at "work."

All the attendees of the ChrisDucker.com Mastermind Sessions around the world, for all their input and support.

And, finally to my online tribe: To every entrepreneur who has ever subscribed to my blog, commented on a post, liked one of my YouTube videos, reviewed my podcast on iTunes, sent me a tweet on Twitter, left me a message on Facebook, come to see me speak live, or e-mailed me to ask questions about how to effectively work with virtual staff. Thank you.

You continue to keep me on my game.

About the Author

Known as the "Virtual CEO" and regarded as the number-one authority on the subject of virtual staffing and personal outsourcing, Chris Ducker is a serial entrepreneur and a native of the UK who has lived in the Philippines since 2000.

Founder and CEO of three businesses, including a call center, a recruitment company, and a co-working space for startup entrepreneurs, Chris is also a popular international keynote speaker, blogger, and podcaster.

Although he has authored many successful e-books in the past, *Virtual Freedom* is Chris' first traditionally published book and the culmination of working with thousands of virtual employees over a ten-year period in the outsourcing industry.

Chris continues to operate his businesses in the Philippines, where he lives with his family, and keeps a busy international travel schedule.

Reach out to him directly on Twitter @chrisducker.

Index

A

accountability, 48, 50, 122
action plans, 146, 220–228
  additional resources and
    miscellaneous links, 261
administrative assistants, 105
AdRoll (Adroll.com), 259
algorithms, 109, 211
Allen, David, 17–18
Amazon (Amazon.com), 224–225
AmyPorterfield.com, 230–231, 262
analytics, 109, 208
Animoto (Animoto.com), 173, 260
app developers, 36–37, 112–114, 161, 175–177
app development tools, 261
articles, 97, 115
Asana (Asana.com), 117, 120, 250, 257
Asian VAs, 249
asking for help, 69
assets, 28, 59, 102, 159–160
Association of Administrative Assistants (AAA.ca), 105
assumptions, 65–69
Audacity (Audacity.sourceforge.net), 260
audio recordings, 77–78, 82

audio/video editors, 161
authority figures, 59
Aweber (Aweber.com), 259

B

Babelverse (Babelverse.com), 258
bad hires, 54, 55
Basecamp (Basecamp.com), 55, 107, 117, 119–120, 250, 257
B2B (business-to-business) Philosophy, 213
B2C (business-to-consumer) Philosophy, 213
Beaumont, Dale, 101
BecomeABlogger (BecomeABlogger.com), 262
being remembered, importance of, 218
benchmarks, 6, 95, 98–100, 117, 182, 191
benefits, 129–130, 181
best practices when training workers, 84–86
Beuckens, Todd, 38–42
bidding, 165
BlogMarketingAcademy (BlogMarketingAcademy.com), 262
blogs. *see also* specific blogs
  3 Lists to Freedom and, 20
  analytics of, 17

content creation of, 207,
213–214, 221
GVAs and, 19
posting to, 85
revolving tasks, 115
Bluehost (Bluehost.com), 261
bonuses, 130–132, 182, 248
boundaries, 69
BPO (business-process
outsourcing), 244
branding, 80, 182, 213, 262
BreakthroughBlogging
(BreakthroughBlogging.com),
259
Breakthrough4Business
(Breakthrough4Business.com),
101–103
BuddyPress (BuddyPress.org),
188, 261
burnout, 3–4
business cards, 19
business growth, 22

C

calendars, 17, 19, 115, 117, 120,
122, 182
Campbell, Anita, 65
Camtasia (Techsmith.com/
Camtasia), 79, 82, 83, 256
career issues, 201
Case Studies
Fiona Lewis, E-Commerce
Business Owner, 144–148
Joshua Van Den Broek,
Principal Exercise
Physiologist, 214–217
Kyle Zimmerman, Fashion
Photographer Turned Studio
Owner, 80–84
Nate Ginsburg, Digital
Nomad, 178–181
Paul Holland, Online
Entrepreneur, 153–156

Steve Dixon, Serial
Entrepreneur, 101–103
Todd Beuckens, Online
Teacher, 38–42
Tom Libelt, Online Service
Provider, 52–55
Tristan King, Location-
Independent Entrepreneur,
70–73
challenges, 69, 86–87, 234
check-in points, 69, 95, 98–99
checklists, 205, 225
chief growth officer (CGO),
190–191
"Chief Happiness Officer," 230
ChrisDucker.com, 7
clerical work, 37
Clickonomics (Cliconomics
.com), 27
common sense, 68
communication
clarity of, 54–55, 216–217
constant, 71–72
daily reporting and
accountability, 48
ease of, 113
face-to-face, 46
lack of proper, 162, 249–250
open line of, 109
proper, 26
respect and, 14
salary and, 128–129
tools of, 257
written instructions, 75–77
company goals, 181–183
compensation, 48, 50, 61,
246–248
competition, 17
confidentiality, 60–62
confrontation, 150
consistency, 203–208
contacts, new, 19
content creation, 200–201,
203–212, 218, 219, 221–224

"content is king," 211
content writers, 33–34, 110–111, 135–136, 161, 170–172
contracts, 60–62
copy editors, 110, 139
copywriters, 135–136
corporate branding, 213
courses, 71, 105, 201, 256
Craigslist (Craigslist.org), 43, 162, 193, 219, 255
creative skills, 203–208
credit cards, 19, 61
CRM (customer relationship Management) content, 61
Croslow, Jared, 27–28
cultural differences, 8, 137, 140, 248–249
customer relationships, 139, 213
customer service, 72, 143
customer support, 133–134, 140–141

D

Daniel, Joe, 188–189
deadlines, 82, 196
DeMarco, MJ, 80
Design Cubicle (TheDesignCubicle.com), 108
99designs (99designs.com), 108
differences, respect for, 249
Digg (Digg.com), 259
digital nomads, 178–181
direction, 96
discounts, 86
Dixon, Steve, 101–103
Dixon Clothing Group, 101–103
Docstoc (Docstoc.com), 259
document sharing, 257
domestic workers, 134–137, 139, 154, 171, 193, 245
downsizing, 193
Dropbox (Dropbox.com)
    minimizing your need for, 119–120

reporting and accountability and, 48
tools and resources, 41–42, 83, 106, 180–181, 257
Dumas, John Lee, 90

E

eaHELP (eaHELP.com), 136, 255
e-books, 223
e-commerce stores, 70
eHarmony, 19
Elance (Elance.com), 43, 99, 107, 159, 164, 255
Elllo (Elllo.org), 38–42
e-mail
    author's, 236
    collaboration via, 184
    filtering, 115
    interviews and, 60
    reporting and accountability, 48
    tasks you don't like doing, 20
    as a tool, 104
    using all caps in, 150
    written instructions and, 75–77
empire-building, 16
Entrepreneur magazine, 105, 109–110
Entrepreneur On Fire, 90
EntrepreneurOnFire (EntrepreneurOnFire.com), 262
environment, 251
equations, 88–90
evaluations, 128
EventualMillionaire (EventualMillionaire.com), 262
evergreen content, 210–211
Evernote (Evernote.com), 111, 258
examples, 95, 97, 165
expectations, 65
experiences, 86, 203
expertise, 65, 87

F

Facebook
  General Virtual Assistants
    (GVAs) and, 19, 67
  marketing and, 230–231
  network for your virtual team
    and, 186–188
  referrals and, 206–208
  revolving tasks, 115
  team-building tools and, 260
face-to-face meetings, 146,
  183–186
FAQs, 85, 87
feedback, 72
Ferriss, Tim, 63
Filipino VAs, 133–134, 137,
  141–143, 148–152
financial questions, 200–201
finding and hiring, 13–62,
  255–256
firing yourself, 4–6
Fitco Health Technologies
  (Fitco.net.au), 214–217
Fiverr (Fiverr.com), 44, 219, 258
Fizzle (Fizzle.co), 259
Flynn, Pat, 4, 91–92
fonts, 108
Football-Defense.com, 188–189
free products, 248
freedom, 95, 99–101
Freedom Spotlight
  Jared Croslow, 27–28
  Joe Daniel, 188–189
  Justin Fulcher, 125–126
  Natalie Sisson, 229–230
  Pat Flynn, 91–92
Freelancer (Freelancer.com), 44,
  255
freelancer marketplace sites,
  44–45
freelancers, 26, 41, 81–83
FreshBooks (FreshBooks.com),
  72, 261
Fulcher, Justin, 125–126

full-time workers, 163–176
functional expertise, 65
fundamentals, 14–15, 233
future growth, 252

G

GarageBand (Apple.com/
  garageband), 260
Garland, David Siteman, 22
General Virtual Assistants (GVAs),
  16–19, 29–30, 103–106, 161,
  162–164, 192, 195, 234–236
Generation Y, 143
Getting Things Done (Allen),
  17–18
gifts, 152
"gig economy," 193
Ginsburg, Nate, 178–181
goals, 6, 89–90, 115, 181–183
good hires, 57
Google, 168, 211
  AdSense, 38, 52
  AdWords, 180, 259
  algorithms, 109
  Analytics, 208
  Drive, 48, 104, 106, 117, 119,
    147, 172, 257
  Google+, 115, 187, 260
  Hangouts, 46, 60, 106, 146,
    147, 184, 257
  Images, 112
  Keyword Tool, 259
  Sites, 147, 217, 257
  Trends, 259
GoToMeeting (GoToMeeting
  .com), 184, 257
graphic designers, 31, 107–108,
  161, 166–168
graphics tools, 261
Great-Web-Design.net, 108
GroupMe (GroupMe.com), 257
growth, 57, 86, 180, 252
Guru.com, 44

H

hardware, 49
health insurance, 129–130
health issues, 200
help, asking for, 69
hierarchy, 196
HireMyMom (HireMyMom.com), 256
hiring
    finding and, 13–62, 255–256
    guides to, 107, 162, 164–165, 166–167, 171
    for the role, 233
    salary guidelines and, 129
HiveDesk (HiveDesk.com), 117, 121, 257
holidays, 128–129, 150–152
Holland, Paul, 153–156
home offices, 105
honesty, 115, 143, 197
The 4-Hour Workweek: Escape 9-5, Live Anywhere, and Join the New Rich (Ferriss), 63
Howes, Lewis, 177
HTML color codes, 108
Hubspot (http://blog.hubspot.com), 107
Huddle (Huddle.com), 257
human interaction, 183–186
Hyatt, Michael, 9

I

iBuildApp (iBuildApp.com), 261
IconArchive (IconArchive.com), 108, 261
IconBeast (IconBeast.com), 113–114, 261
IFTTT Cheat Sheet, 85–86
image libraries, 108, 261
Inc. magazine, 107
incentives, 130–132
independents, 81
infographics, 166–167

innovation, 2
Instagram (Instagram.com), 260
insurance, health, 129–130
interaction between virtual assistants, 160–168
interviews, 54, 55–60, 129, 169, 193–195
introductions, 184
iStock (iStockPhoto.com), 108, 261

J

JamesWedmore.com, 213–214, 262
Jing (Techsmith.com/Jing), 55, 79, 103, 156, 256
job descriptions, 47–51, 61
job titles, 47, 50
job-by-job basis, 81–82
job-posting sites, 43–44, 47, 60
"just in time" model, 27

K

key loggers, 241–242
keywords, 108–109, 115, 169, 170
Kinda IT, 125–126
King, Tristan, 70–73
KPO (knowledge-process outsourcing), 244
Kyle Zimmerman Photography, 80–84

L

LastPass (LastPass.com), 61, 258
lawyers, 60
LeadPages (LeadPages.net), 259
learning from your virtual assistants, 180
legal action, 60–61
Lewis, Fiona, 144–148
LewisHowes.com, 262

Libelt, Tom, 52–55

Libelty SEO (LibeltySEO.com), 52–55

"Life is art" slogan, 80

LinkedIn (LinkedIn.com), 115, 187, 260

Live2Sell, Inc., 3–4

local businesses, 205–206

local events, 17

local workers. *See* domestic workers

location, choosing the wrong, 244

Location Rebel(LocationRebel .com), 71

Long Tail Pro (LongTailPro.com), 110, 259

loyalty, 59, 182–183

Lynda (Lynda.com), 71, 256

M

Market Samurai (MarketSamurai .com), 110, 259

marketing
  "gurus," 247
  Lewis Howes and, 177
  Nate Ginsburg and, 179
  ongoing, 219, 227–228
  online, 21
  proofreading and, 171
  strategies, 169
  tools, 259–260

Mashable (Mashable.com), 113

Match (Match.com), 19

MeetingBurner (MeetingBurner .com), 257

meetings, 115, 184

Mentoring Mums Online, 144

mentorship, 144, 203

MichaelHyatt.com, 262

micromanagement, 4–5, 94–95, 100, 125, 237, 241–243

Microtask (Microtask.com), 258

milestones, 120, 234

The Millionaire Fastlane (DeMarco), 80

Mind Tools (MindTools.com), 105, 256

Mindjet (Mindjet.com), 154, 156, 257

mismanagement, 239–244

mistakes, 72, 93–94, 243

mobile app developers. *See* app developers

mobile app development tools, 261

MobileDevHQ (MobileDevHQ .com), 113, 261

mockups, 72

money, 18, 139, 152, 196

most valuable commodity (MVC), 18

motivation, 122, 126–132, 139

MumPreneurs Online: Exposed (Lewis), 144

MumPreneursOnline.com, 144

music, 97, 112

MyExercisePhysiologist.com, 215

N

NDAs (Nondisclosure Agreements), 62

needs of virtual assistants, 244–245

The New York Times, 63

NewBusinessPodcast.com, 7

ninety-day action plans, 146

99Designs (99designs.com), 258

Ning (Ning.com), 187, 260

O

objectives, 95–96, 98–99

oDesk (oDesk.com), 43, 99, 159, 164, 178, 180, 256

office requirements, 8, 105

Ogle, Sean, 71
online stores, 205–206
Onset LLC (OnsetLLC.com),
  178–181
operational guidelines document,
  88, 196, 250
order fulfillment, 84
organizations, roles in, 25
outdated material, 211–212
outsourcing
  agencies, 146
  companies for, 42–43
  cost-saving benefits of, 8
  Fiona Lewis and, 145
  following the wrong model
    for, 245–246
  one-off solutions, 258
  Paul Holland and, 153–154
  training system for, 24–26
  why it may not be for you,
    138–140
  your understanding and,
    253–254
overseas workers, 8, 133–134,
  171

P

Parker, Peter, 1
part-time workers, 163, 174
payments, 130, 150, 258–259
PayPal (PayPal.com), 61, 130,
  259
payroll, 104, 126–132
personal assistants (PA), 18
personality, 57, 192
Philippines, workers from. *See*
  Filipino VAs
Pinterest (Pinterest.com), 260
plagiarism, 111, 259
Plagiarism Checker
(PlagiarismChecker.com), 111,
  259
Plato, 4

plugins, 106
podcasts, 7, 260–261
Porterfield, Amy, 230–231
portfolios, 166
potential, 57
power, responsibility and, 1–2
PowerPoint, 71
P2P (People-to-People)
  Philosophy, 212–214, 218, 219
prejudice, 251
press, 17, 207
pricing, 86
priorities, 89, 90
privacy, 120
production, process to, 95–101
productivity, 16–17, 184, 258
profanity, 86
professional videos, 207
professionals, 22
progress, 95
project management, 107,
  117–121, 118–121, 194
project-management software,
  118–121, 154, 250, 256–257
project managers, 189–197
project-based outsourcing, 25,
  43–44, 107, 166
projects, 96, 117–118
promotions, 219, 225–227, 252
publication, 221–224
purchasing, 19, 84, 86

Q

quality of work, 14, 233
quarterly tasks, 49
questionnaires, 73–74
questions, 122, 123, 139
Quick-start SEO, 109–110

R

raises, 248
rapport, 58–59, 78, 129, 149

recommendations, 87
recruitment, 45–46, 192–193, 253
Reddit (Reddit.com), 259
referrals, 183, 206
religious beliefs, 143, 150–152
repetitive tasks, 16–17, 179–180
reporting and accountability, 48, 50, 121–124, 131, 169
reputation, 143
research, 19, 85, 115, 219, 220
resources, 104–108, 111–114, 119–121, 147–148, 156, 255–263, 255–263
respect for workers, 14, 127–128
response time, 38
responsibility, 1–2, 65, 72
reviews, 208
revolving tasks, 114–116
rewards, 181–182, 181–183
RhinoSupport (RhinoSupport .com), 258
Risley, David, 46
role-based outsourcing, 25–26
rush jobs, 82
RyanLee.com, 262

S

salary guidelines, 126–132
  app developers, 36
  average, 53
  content writers, 33
  general virtual assistants (GVAs), 29
  gifts and, 152
  graphic designers, 31
  holidays, 128–129
  increase in, 128
  negotiation of, 60
  SEO (Search Engine Optimization)/Internet Marketing VAs, 32
  vacation, 128–129

video editors, 35
  web developers, 30
Samuel, Leslie, 9
ScheduleOnce (ScheduleOnce .com), 258
Schramko, James, 21
Screencast (Screencast.com), 41, 257
screencasts, 78–79
ScreenFlow (Telestream.net /ScreenFlow), 79, 256
screenshots, 72, 76, 121, 242
scripts, 112
search engines, 168
security, sense of, 59
self-awareness, 243–244
self-employment, 129–130. 193
self-teaching, 203
selling, 20
SEO glossary (SEOBook.com /Glossary), 109
SEO (Search Engine Optimization)/Internet Marketing VA, 31–33, 71, 108–110, 161, 168–170, 235
Shalwick, Gideon, 112
Shopify Ninjas (ShopifyNinjas .com), 70–73
Shopify (Shopify.com), 260
ShoutEm (Shoutem.com), 113, 261
Simplenote (Simplenote.com), 111, 258
Sisson, Natalie, 9, 229–230
six-month timeline, 234–236
skills
  attention to, 139
  creative, 203–208
  daily work description and, 49
  difficult, 49–50
  hiring and, 57–58, 165
  improvement of, 58–59
  job descriptions and, 48
  new, 87

technical, 203–208
training and, 65
Skype (Skype.com)
  communication and, 72,
    214–217
  feedback and, 73
  interviews and, 45–46, 60,
    194
  language and tone and, 150
  meetings on, 184
  tools and resources, 55, 83,
    106, 156, 180, 257
  training and, 78
SlideShare (SlideShare.net), 260
slogans, 80
Small Business Trends
  (SmallBizTrends.com), 65, 262
small businesses, 133, 157
Smart Passive Income, 4, 91–92
smartphones, 205–206
Snagit (Techsmith.com/Snagit),
  147–148, 256
social media, 7, 17, 46, 85,
  115–116, 260. *see also* specific
  sites
social networks, 186–188
software, 49, 117, 118–121, 167.
  See also specific software
solopreneurship, 95, 196, 215
solutions, 88
Spider-Man, 1
Splasheo (Splasheo.com), 112,
  261
spouses, 19
startups, 133
stores, 205–206
storyboard templates, 112
strengths and weaknesses, 14
structure, 249–250
StumbleUpon (StumbleUpon
  .com), 260
success, measurement of, 65,
  88–90
suggested reading, 262–263

Suitcase Entrepreneur
  (SuitcaseEntrepreneur.com),
  229–230, 262
Super Savvy Business
  (SuperSavvyBusiness.com),
  144–148
SuperFastBusiness
  (SuperFastBusiness.com), 21,
  262
superhero syndrome, 1–3, 5, 7,
  18, 94–95, 113, 121, 123, 237
super-VA, 15–16, 233
surveys, 87
syncing, 257

T

talents, 86, 251–253
Tardy, Jaime, 21
tasks
  assignment of, 195–196
  checklist for, 205
  daily work description and,
    49, 50–51
  freedom from, 20–24
  low-level, 22
  meaningful, 103
  measurement of, 96
  mentality of, 159
  revolving, 84–85, 114–116
  showdown of, 114
  you don't know how to do, 21
  you don't like doing, 20–21
  you feel you shouldn't be
    doing, 22–23
taxes, 130
teaching, online, 38–42
teambuilding, 160, 197, 260
teams
  breaking down, 7
  building, 7, 16, 24–25
  "company first" mentality and,
    181
  fitting roles into, 163–177

power of, 191

training, 25

treatment of, 155

Teamwork Project Management (TeamworkPM.net), 103, 120, 257

technical skills, 203–208

TeuxDeux (TeuxDeux.com), 258

TheBestDesigns.com, 108

TheRiseToTheTop.com, 22, 262

ThinkTraffic (ThinkTraffic.net), 263

3 Lists to Freedom, 20–24, 28, 65, 234, 236, 245

throwing a curveball, 86–88

time, 18, 69, 127, 202–203

time zones, 8, 48, 70, 85, 135, 162, 185

TimeandDate (TimeandDate.com /holidays), 258

timelines, 234–236

tone, 150

tools and resources, 104–108, 111–114, 119–121, 147–148, 156, 255–263

training

    assumptions and, 65–68

    best practices, 84–86

    communication and, 71–72, 73

    defining the role, 65

    failure to properly, 25

    for General Virtual Assistants (GVAs), 105

    importance of, 89, 90

    intentional, 73

    investing in, 251

    offering opportunities for, 146–147

    problems with, 64–65

    recorded, 77–79, 82

    setting expectations, 65

    skill areas, 71

    time and money for, 253

    tools of, 256

written instructions, 75–77

transcription, 17, 224

treatment of virtual assistants, 155, 216–217

Trello (Trello.com), 72, 217, 258

trial periods, 162

trust, 129

Twitter (Twitter.com), 7, 46, 115, 260

U

Udemy (Udemy.com), 256

understanding your company, 253–254

V

"VA for hire" services, 44

VA Success Equation, 88–90

VA Training Trifecta, 74–75

value of virtual assistants, 103

Van Den Broek, Joshua, 214–217

video creation, 222, 260–261

video editors, 34–36, 111–112, 160, 173–175

video recordings, 78–79, 211

VideoTise, 153–156

virtual assistants

    app developers, 36–37, 112–114, 161, 175–177

    audio/video editors, 161

    best practices when training your, 84–86

    clerical work, 37

    content writers, 33–34, 110–111, 135–136, 161, 170–172

    domestic, 134–137, 139, 154, 171, 193, 245

    expertise of, 65

    failures with using, 24–25

    Filipino, 133–134, 137, 141–143, 148–152

finding and hiring, 13–62,
255–256
General Virtual Assistants
(GVAs), 16–19, 29–30,
103–106, 161, 162–164,
192, 195, 234–236
getting to know your, 73–74
graphic designers, 31,
107–108, 161, 166–168
interaction between, 160–168
learning from your, 180
needs of, 244–245
overseas, 8, 133–134, 171
questionnaire for, 73–74
SEO (Search Engine
Optimization)/Internet
Marketing VA, 31–33, 71,
108–110, 161, 168–170,
235
treatment of, 155, 216–217
types of, 28–36
value of, 103
video editors, 34–36, 111–
112, 160, 173–175
web developers, 21, 30–31,
106–107, 161, 164–166
Virtual Business Lifestyle, 5
Virtual CEO, 3–6, 95
virtual courses, 71
Virtual Staff Finder
(VirtualStaffFinder.com), 6–7,
15, 45, 50–51, 136–137, 141,
256
Virtual Staff Training Academy
(VirtualStaffTrainingAcademy
.com), 256
virtual teams, 8–9
virtual vultures, 94–95, 100
vision, 2, 64, 146, 253

W

web developers, 21, 30–31,
106–107, 161, 164–166

web development tools, 261
webcam trainings, 79
web-design terms, 107
Web2Explosion (Web2Explosion
.com), 112
Wedmore, James, 213–214
Western Union, 130, 152
white papers, 221, 223
whiteboards, 184
word counts, 110
word processing, 71
WordPress (WordPress.com), 34,
79, 164, 188, 205, 246, 253,
261
work descriptions, 49
work ethic, 87, 101, 143, 248
work history, 60, 121
workspaces, 105, 149
WPCurve (WPCurve.com), 261
written instructions, 75–77

X

Xero (Xero.com), 262

Y

Yammer (Yammer.com), 186,
187, 188, 260
YouTube (YouTube.com), 7, 19,
97, 170, 213–214, 261

Z

ZenDesk (Zendesk.com), 257
Zimmerman, Kyle, 9, 80–84
Zirtual (Zirtual.com), 136, 256